On Satan, Demons, and Psychiatry

On Satan, Demons, and Psychiatry

Exploring Mental Illness in the Bible

RAGY R. GIRGIS, M.D.

WIPF & STOCK · Eugene, Oregon

ON SATAN, DEMONS, AND PSYCHIATRY
Exploring Mental Illness in the Bible

Wipf & Stock
An Imprint of Wipf and Stock Publishers
199 W. 8th Ave., Suite 3
Eugene, OR 97401

www.wipfandstock.com

PAPERBACK ISBN: 978-1-5326-9989-4
HARDCOVER ISBN: 978-1-5326-9990-0
EBOOK ISBN: 978-1-5326-9991-7

Manufactured in the U.S.A.

Contents

CHAPTER 1

Preface and Introduction

Mr. S was a twenty-three-year-old male from a middle-class family. He was casually groomed, wearing jeans and a T-shirt. He used advanced grammar, had a calm demeanor, always smiled, and demonstrated very good manners, saying "please" and "thank you" as well as "sir" and "ma'am" whenever addressing people older than him, including me, the psychiatrist, whom he was seeing for a consultation.

Mr. S's father was a petroleum engineer and his mother was a homemaker. He had one older sister and a younger brother. They were raised in a very strict and conservative Presbyterian household. The family prayed before every meal, first thing in the morning, and last thing at night. They attended church on a weekly basis.

I was seeing Mr. S as his psychiatrist and parents were concerned about symptoms he was experiencing and that were troubling to him. Namely, he described a feeling that he was receiving messages from angels about predicting the future, as well as fears that some evil spirits had possessed his pet cat in order to monitor him. Mr. S was not fully convinced that he was receiving messages from angels or that his cat was possessed, but thought that it may be possible. These symptoms were distressing to him but did not affect his functioning. In fact, he had graduated as the valedictorian of his high school class and was socially and otherwise interpersonally very successful.

He was referred to me by his psychiatrist given my expertise in early and developing psychotic disorders. After a forty-five-minute interview with Mr. S and his parents it became clear that Mr. S was experiencing attenuated psychotic symptoms. Attenuated psychotic symptoms are symptoms that are similar to delusions and hallucinations that one may experience in a psychotic disorder such as schizophrenia, but with less than full conviction. People who have these types of symptoms are considered to be at high risk for psychosis. Namely, they have an approximately 30 percent chance of developing a full psychotic disorder, such as schizophrenia.[1]

I began to explain my findings and clinical impression to Mr. S and his parents. I asked him from where he believed his thoughts were coming, to which he replied, "The messages from the angels are coming from God and the spirits that have possessed my cat are coming from the devil." In fact, all of Mr. S's understanding of his condition was that his distressing symptoms were from either God or Satan and may or may not have been true, but seemed reasonable. Despite fifteen more minutes of trying to help Mr. S understand the nature of his condition (i.e., that it was not spiritual in nature but related to psychiatry and biology), I made no progress. Mr. S interpreted all of his symptoms as spiritual in nature, in one manner or another.

Mr. S's psychiatrist had prescribed a medication for psychotic symptoms called risperidone, which decreased the intensity of the symptoms. I suggested to Mr. S that if a medication such as risperidone had decreased his symptoms, would that not suggest that his thoughts were biological rather than spiritual in nature, to which he politely responded, "I really do not see how that makes any difference."

1. Fusar-Poli et al., "Psychosis High-risk State," 107–20.

The lay, and sometimes professional (i.e., clergy), view of serious mental illness by Christian believers is frequently one of moral weakness, bad parenting, and volition. This view is born from images of homeless people, drug abusers, media portrayals of mass murders, and the entertainment industry's exploitation of mental illness for dramatic purposes. In addition, many are under the false understanding that serious mental illness is a recent (i.e., within the last half century) phenomenon and is not consistent with a Christian worldview. Many people simply equate any bad or undesirable behavior with mental illness. Finally, as in the case of Mr. S, many reject that serious mental illness is non-spiritual and biologically-based. These misconceptions often prevent Christian believers with serious mental illness and their families from seeking professional mental health treatment when it is most needed. In many cases, they do not accept psychiatric medications as they would medications for non-psychiatric conditions, such as high blood pressure or diabetes.

Therefore, the goal of this book is to help change misconceptions that have historically pervaded Christianity by educating both laity and clergy about serious mental illness. I will accomplish this goal via an in-depth, exegetic examination of Biblical accounts of what may have been untreated serious mental illness from the perspective of a Christian psychiatrist. I will also examine other stories from the Bible that could reveal a great deal of information about the Biblical view of mental illness that may be helpful to patients with serious mental illness, their families, and anyone interested in this topic. This in-depth examination will demonstrate that 1) serious mental illness was likely present and relatively common in Biblical times, and similar in phenomenology to how it manifests today, and 2) that some instances of demon possession and exorcisms as described in the Bible could, in a post-Enlightenment narrative, be better explained by occurring in the context of untreated mental illness, and that this could reveal a great deal of information about the Biblical view of mental illness. Some of these accounts are from the Old Testament and some from the New Testament. Each essay will provide an in-depth examination of the Biblical account from the perspective of a board-certified psychiatrist who is an expert in the field of serious mental illness and who is also a practicing Christian. I will go through each of the selected Bible accounts in detail, making the reader aware of what suggests that the story may be about mental illness or how understanding the story in the context of mental illness could enhance the message of the story. This first chapter will present this thesis and the concluding chapter will provide guidance on how understanding the selected Bible stories from the perspective of serious mental illness affects the messages of these stories.

Importantly, this book will focus on serious mental illnesses such as severe depression, bipolar disorder, and schizophrenia, for several reasons. First, although there remains substantial stigma related to all types of mental illness, Christian communities, and society as a whole, have made substantial advances in their understanding and acceptance of other forms of mental illness, in part related to how common they are. In contrast, serious mental illness is much less understood and much more stigmatized by society than other forms of mental illness. This is in part because serious mental illness is much less common, but also because the behavior observed in these conditions, when untreated, is often so different and at times bizarre compared to what is considered typical human behavior that many people, not only Christian believers, have a much harder time understanding these conditions. To be clear, illnesses such as anxiety and other disorders not typically classified as "serious mental illness" and not discussed as much in this book are often extremely severe and debilitating, though for this book we will focus on schizophrenia and related psychotic disorders, bipolar disorder, and severe forms of depression.

There are several books about mental illness and Christianity or the Bible in general. Many of these are very good, though have very different objectives than my objective in the current book. For example, other books generally focus on other forms of mental illness, or only focus on negative emotional states such as loneliness, as opposed to serious mental illness. They also tend to focus on metaphysical, abstract, philosophical, or theological arguments and discussions about living life as a Christian with other forms of mental illness, with a specific focus on general emotional states, rather than on the details of specific stories and narratives in the Bible and how they relate to mental illness. Many spend much time discussing what it means to have negative emotional states as a Christian. Some other very good books also deal more specifically with educating people who minister to Christian believers about mental illness and therefore focus more on introducing the audience to the basics of mental illness, including its modern history, the criteria for each disorder, and how the medications work, etc. Some books focus on general emotional issues and how to minister to Christians with mental illness. Sometimes these books use biographical examples in which the authors describe their own experiences with mental illness. These books are very good and make some references to stories from the Bible, but in no cases do these books deal with Biblical stories of serious mental illness and theology in the depth and level of examination that I undertake in the current book.

These other books are very good and serve important purposes. However, the purpose of this book is unique. The complete focus of this book is on Bible stories and interpreting and understanding them in a post-Enlightenment narrative, from the perspective of serious mental illness (i.e., schizophrenia and related psychotic disorders, bipolar disorder, and severe depression), using an exegetic technique, similar to a commentary written from the perspective of a psychiatrist. For this book, I will go through each of the selected Bible stories in great detail, making the reader aware of what suggests that the stories could also be understood as being about untreated serious mental illness and how understanding the stories in the context of serious mental illness could enhance their meaning. Since mental illness is so common and likely a problem encountered by many people including primarily laity, but also clergy and academicians, I, in this book, as demonstrated by the examples provided herein, use language and a style that make the explanations and interpretations more accessible to the reader, closer to a narrative prose rather than a more formal commentary. To this end, I have also limited the use of references outside of references to the Bible and a limited number of scientific articles or texts.

While other books offer readers emotional insights into accepting other forms of mental illness as a Christian, they primarily focus on other forms of mental illness, or just focus on "negative" emotional states, such as loneliness. While less common than other forms of mental illness, serious mental illnesses remain very prevalent (~3–5 percent of the adult population).[2] In addition, other books do not serve the main objective of this book of using accounts of individuals in the Bible who could also be understood as having untreated serious mental illness to teach that these are serious mental health conditions that require psychiatric treatment and can be successfully treated. Most people know at least one person afflicted with serious mental illness. Unfortunately, because of the substantial stigma associated with serious mental illness, most people usually simply ignore these conditions or have other, less accurate ideas about them. This leads those people closest to serious mental illness feeling lost as to how to understand what they or their family member or friend is going through. This book is being written specifically with these individuals in mind, giving very practical, specific examples about what may be serious mental illness in the Bible. I will also examine other stories from the Bible that may be better explained by mental illness and could reveal a great deal of information about the Biblical view of mental illness that may be helpful to patients with serious mental illness, their families, and anyone interested in this topic. These examples will allow readers to arm themselves with the knowledge of potential Biblical examples of untreated serious mental illness as well as an enhanced Biblical understanding of serious mental illness. Similar to the goal of apologetics, this knowledge will give Christian believers with serious mental illness, or who have family or friends with serious mental illness, the confidence to understand and defend their own or their loved one's condition as being

2. Substance Use and Mental Health Services Administration, "Key Substance Use."

consistent with a Christian worldview. Finally, my own academic and clinical expertise is in serious mental illness, which allows me a unique perspective on, and understanding of, these conditions.

By discussing well-known Biblical stories with accompanying explanations of what these stories reveal about serious mental illness, the reader will gain an appreciation of the non-morality- and non-spirituality-based, biological nature and timelessness of serious mental illness, and for the therapeutic potential of currently available treatments. Importantly, great strides have been made in the treatment of serious mental illness. Therefore, this book will conclude with a message of hope and good news for those with serious mental illness or for those with family members with mental illness, emphasizing the successes of modern treatments and good prognoses these individuals now have—prognoses that could not be offered in a world in which demon possession and exorcism are considered the drivers of mental illness.

Very importantly, my goal in this book is not to change the readers' views of the Bible stories presented herein, but rather to use the Bible to enhance what we understand about serious mental illness. For example, while some characters in the Bible who are discussed below, such as King Saul, Jonah, and Nebuchadnezzar, were more clearly described as having symptoms consistent with untreated mental illness, others, such as the individuals in chapters 8 and 9 who were described as demon-possessed and were healed by Jesus Christ, were not described as having mental illness. My hope is that, rather than changing how we understand the stories and miracles, examining them in the context of serious mental illness can reveal to us the Biblical understanding of serious mental illness.

In particular, after a brief introduction to serious mental illness (chapter 2), I will, in chapter 3, review and discuss how Moses described and used serious mental illness as a consequence of disobedience to God. In chapter 5 I will present how King David feigned psychosis, suggesting the relative commonality of this behavior and a general understanding of the presence of psychosis during his time.

In chapters 4, 6, and 7 I will examine the symptoms of serious mental illness experienced by King Saul, Jonah, and Nebuchadnezzar. I also discuss the severe depression, and at times suicidality, experienced by Moses, Naomi, Jeremiah, Job, and Elijah.

In chapters 8 and 9 I will present two of the miracles performed by Jesus Christ that are described as exorcisms. In both cases, I will describe in detail how considering the behavior of the afflicted individuals in the context of untreated serious mental illness can enhance our understanding of these stories. I will discuss how mental illness was conceptualized and described in Biblical times and use the stories of Adam and Eve and Job to clarify the extent to which God allows Satan to affect humankind. Chapter 9 also includes a direct examination of exorcisms, both in Biblical and modern times. Chapter 9 ends with a discussion about how understanding the miracles of Jesus Christ from chapters 8 and 9 in the context of serious mental illness enhances their message and reveals a great deal about the Biblical understanding of serious mental illness.

Very importantly, many people who have read earlier versions of this book have told me that it is somewhat challenging to try to understand chapters 8 and 9 through the lens of serious mental illness because that could suggest that two miracles of Jesus Christ that have always been considered to be exorcisms and demon possession could potentially be the healing of mental illness. Some also suggest that the interpretation of serious mental illness "takes away" from these miracles. I would suggest that this additional understanding actually enhances our understanding of these miracles and, more importantly, of how we should understand serious mental illness. I would like to emphasize that the categories of mental illness described in this book are modern categories that reflect post-Enlightenment rationality. The Bible comes from a different narrative culture that could not explain things in terms of Enlightenment rationality. For example, many of the stories in chapters 8 and 9 about exorcisms and demon possession reflect the narrative of the ancient world. From the perspective of modern rationality, we understand these individuals' behavior in a different way—perhaps as serious mental illness. When reading this book and understanding the Bible stories, one must recognize that these two narratives (pre- and post-Enlightenment) produce two narrative assumptions that are different but readily and largely overlap. If we keep clear about the two different rationalities we can honor them both. This, however, requires of us an honest recognition that the two narrative perspectives are not incommensurate, and we, as believers, are in some way participants in both worlds. It is imperative on us, if we are going to make any progress towards dealing with serious mental illness and stigma, to work at seeing how these two narratives relate and illuminate each other, rather than to adjudicate on the truth of these stories.

Further, I would like to use another miracle of Jesus Christ to further clarify what he says about how we should interpret and understand his miracles. In a very well-known story as told in Mark 2, Luke 5, and Matthew 9, Jesus was preaching in a house. The house was very full. Several men had a friend who was paralyzed and whom they wanted to set before Jesus. Since they were unable to enter the house through the doorway, they lowered him through the roof. Jesus, seeing their persistence and faith, forgave the paralyzed man's sins. The Pharisees and other teachers began to think very critically of Jesus, upset that he was, in their opinion, blaspheming God by forgiving sins. Jesus sensed their thoughts and asked them whether they thought that it would be easier to forgive someone's sins or cure their paralysis. In order to demonstrate that Jesus has dominion over all things heavenly and earthly, Jesus then healed the paralytic man, to the amazement of everyone in attendance.

Another example is at the resurrection of Lazarus of Bethany described in John 11. Initially, Jesus and his disciples were sent word by Lazarus's sisters Mary and Martha that Lazarus was ill. Jesus waited two days then decided to go to Judea to "awaken" Lazarus. The disciples told Jesus that it would be good for Lazarus to sleep in order to recover from his illness. They also did not want Jesus to go to Judea out of concern for his safety. They very clearly still did not understand who Jesus really is and why he had to go to Judea. Therefore, Jesus said,

> "Our friend Lazarus has fallen asleep; but I am going there to wake him up." His disciples replied, "Lord, if he sleeps, he will get better." Jesus had been speaking of his death, but his disciples thought he meant natural sleep. So then he told them plainly, "Lazarus is dead, and for your sake I am glad I was not there, so that you may believe. But let us go to him." (vv. 11–15)

Jesus knew that he had to raise Lazarus from the dead to enhance the faith of his disciples whom he would soon leave on Earth and whom would continue his ministry to humankind.

When Jesus arrived, he saw how sad everyone was, including the townspeople, Martha, and Mary. To Martha he said,

> "Your brother will rise again." Martha answered, "I know he will rise again in the resurrection at the last day." Jesus said to her, "I am the resurrection and the life. The one who believes in me will live, even though they die; and whoever lives by believing in me will never die. Do you believe this?" "Yes, Lord," she replied, "I believe that you are the Messiah, the Son of God, who is to come into the world." (vv. 23–27)

Shortly thereafter, Mary said to Jesus, "Lord, if you had been here, my brother would not have died" (v. 32). As the disciples still did not understand who Jesus is, Martha and Mary did not understand the power of Jesus Christ. After being asked to see where Lazarus's body had been placed, "Jesus wept" (v. 35).

These two words are some of the most powerful words in the Bible and some of the most meaningful. After seeing Jesus in tears, the people who were present remarked, "See how he loved him!" (v. 36), implying that Jesus was tearful because he was sad that Lazarus had died. However, the real meaning of Jesus's tears is made apparent by the next four verses (vv. 37–40):

> But some of them said, "Could not he who opened the eyes of the blind man have kept this man from dying?"

> Jesus, once more deeply moved, came to the tomb. It was
> a cave with a stone laid across the entrance. "Take away
> the stone," he said. "But, Lord," said Martha, the sister of
> the dead man, "by this time there is a bad odor, for he has
> been there four days." Then Jesus said, "Did I not tell you
> that if you believe, you will see the glory of God?"

Jesus was not tearful because he missed Lazarus. What
these verses clarify is that Jesus was tearful because the disciples,
Martha, Mary, and the townspeople, despite all of Jesus' miracles
and everything he had done, still had no understanding of who
Jesus is. They were focused on a physical understanding of the
situation and of Jesus, rather than on a spiritual understanding.

The relevance of this story to the current discussion is that
many times we, believers, fall victim to believing physical phenomena more than the true, supernatural teachings and attributes
of Jesus and his message. In this story, Jesus is clearly trying to
teach everyone present and who reads the story for all time that
healing a paralytic person, or any other physical miracle, is not
in and of itself the message of Jesus Christ but meant to enhance
the true message, miracle, and story of Jesus Christ—namely, that
Jesus Christ was crucified and rose from the dead on the third day
to abolish our sins, thereby giving eternal life to all who believe
in him. Of course Jesus Christ exorcised demons and Satan, in
the greatest way possible. He allowed himself to be crucified and
then resurrected. All other miracles, phenomena, and stories are
meant to confirm and lead us to this revelation. The true miracle,
or "exorcism" if you will, performed by Jesus is his resurrection
and subsequent victory over death, not his casting out of spirits
or healing people who are blind or have other physical or mental
conditions. I would urge the reader to keep this important story
and point in mind as you read through chapters 8 and 9.

While all previous chapters have based their discussions on
one particular Bible story, chapters 10 and 11 focus less on a specific Bible passage and more on the sum total of what the Bible
says about the topics of sorcery, spirits, witchcraft, Satan, and
other supernatural phenomena not directly related to God, Jesus,

the Holy Spirit, or the disciples. What the Bible says about these phenomena is unambiguous and supports the thesis of this book in an important way. While not directly speaking to mental illness as all of the previous chapters did, the passages in the Bible about these phenomena do directly address how we should interpret exorcisms and spiritual healing. In particular, chapter 10 comprehensively reviews all of the additional references to witchcraft, magic, or related spiritual behavior in the Bible and considers what the authors of the Bible say about them.

In chapter 11, I review how the Bible explains that only God has power over Creation, and that Satan works through temptation, or spiritual demon possession, using tools such as lies, deceit, pride, haughtiness, and trickery. The Bible is clear that Satan is very powerful, evil is real, and all believers should be mindful and watchful for temptation. However, the Bible is equally clear that, since Jesus Christ blessed humankind with his incarnation, so much so that we share a holy nature with God, Satan cannot and could never infiltrate a person's body or directly control their mind.

Chapter 12 is substantially more philosophical, theological, and metaphysical than any of the other chapters in this book. It is an exegesis about the end of the world and a discussion about how what the Bible says about the end of the world can shed light on demon possession and serious mental illness.

The final chapter, chapter 13, collates all of the previous discussions and examples and examines how they support the central thesis of this book. This chapter ends with a reflection on the importance of the knowledge gained from an examination of exorcisms, demon possession, and serious mental illness in the Bible and how this knowledge is relevant to people with a Christian worldview.

In the epilogue, I will briefly address two important matters related to the thesis and topic of this book. The first matter is the phenomenon of "voices," "conversations," and other experiences that Christian believers describe as having with God. The second point, about which I am very frequently asked by my patients, is whether people with serious mental illness, such as psychotic disorders, or other disorders that ravage a person's mind, such as Alzheimer's disease, and can make a person act in an ostensibly sinful way or just ignore Jesus Christ, can be saved.

My objective is for this book to be a resource for any Christian, including both the lay believer as well as clergy and Christian academicians (e.g., theologians, students in Christian religion-based fields). I find that many Christian believers, including both laity and clergy, have misconceptions about serious mental illness, such as that it is related to moral weakness, bad parenting, and/or volition. In addition, many are under the false understanding that serious mental illness is a recent (i.e., within the last half century) phenomenon and is not consistent with a Christian worldview. Finally, many reject that serious mental illness is non-spiritual and biologically-based. These misconceptions often prevent Christian believers with serious mental illness and their families from seeking professional mental-health treatment when it is most needed. In many cases, they do not accept psychiatric medications as they would medications for non-psychiatric conditions, such as high blood pressure or diabetes. This is not to say that prayer and faith have no role in the healing of serious mental health. Rather, prayer and faith have a role in every aspect of our lives, including serious mental illness, and I encourage my patients of faith to rely heavily on these aspects of their lives. Rather, I would suggest that believing that serious mental illness is primarily volitional and related to moral weakness, rather than biological in nature and no different than high blood pressure, diabetes, or cancer, does a disservice to individuals with serious mental illness and their families. I am writing this book with the express motivation to change these misconceptions and help readers to understand that serious mental illness is real and not inconsistent with a Christian worldview.

Therefore, the goal of this book is to help change misconceptions that have historically pervaded Christianity by educating both laity and clergy about serious mental illness. I hope to provide an engaging yet educational account of untreated serious mental illness in Biblical times, with the ultimate objective of decreasing stigma about serious mental illness in the Christian community and increasing acceptance of psychiatric treatment. Further, although there is often a nihilism associated with serious mental illness, I aim to instill hope and realistic expectations in patients and their family members/friends who may have much less experience with serious mental illness and harbor very discouraged views on life with serious mental illness. These individuals often pray for "miracles" to help their family/friends, without understanding that medical treatment can be part of God's will. I also believe that any mental health practitioner who treats individuals from a Judeo-Christian background, as well as any individual from a Judeo-Christian background, would potentially benefit from, and be interested in, components of this book.

Finally, to introduce myself, why I am writing this book, and my qualifications for doing so, I am an associate professor of clinical psychiatry at the Columbia University department of psychiatry and New York State Psychiatric Institute. I am primarily an academic researcher, focusing on serious mental illness, and in particular schizophrenia, with a focus on brain imaging as well as the development of experimental treatments. I have published approximately seventy peer-reviewed journal articles and several scientific book chapters pertaining to treatment and the neurobiology of schizophrenia. However, in addition to my research, I am board certified and keep a very high clinical caseload, seeing approximately four to five thousand patients every year, the majority of them with serious mental illness. Please note that, while the clinical anecdotes described in this book are informed by my extensive clinical experience, all clinical anecdotes and patient descriptions are fictional and do not refer to any patient or person I have ever treated in any capacity. The anecdotes are simply meant to enhance the reader's understanding of the material presented in this book.

I have wanted to write this book for over a decade ever since I entered my training in psychiatry in 2005. However, for a number of reasons, I was only able to write it recently. The two main reasons are that it took years to develop the expertise and understanding in serious mental illness to be able to write a book for a lay population. In addition, I realized that, for many years, I had not read near enough theology, and did not know enough about the Bible, to present an adequate commentary. While I still have much to learn, over the several years before writing this book I immersed myself in Christian and Biblical theology, so that I had enough of a background to be able to write this book.

I am also a practicing Christian. I have been very active throughout my life in my church on numerous levels, including as a Sunday school teacher and head deacon. I have given many lectures and seminars on mental illness in the Bible to different faith-based communities. My experiences with individuals with mental illness, Christian believers, and their families are ultimately what led me to write this book, with the goals of helping the reader to gain an appreciation of the non-morality- and non-spirituality-based, biological nature and timelessness of serious mental illness, and for the therapeutic potential of currently available treatments.

CHAPTER 2

A Brief Summary
of Serious Mental Illness

———————

As described in Chapter 1, this book will focus primarily on serious mental illness. Therefore, this chapter will provide a very brief overview of serious mental illness. Serious mental illness has several definitions, though is generally designated by the degree and length of disability that it produces. Serious mental illness is often associated with psychosis. Psychosis is defined as a disconnection from reality and is one source of commonality among serious mental illness. Psychotic symptoms include delusions, hallucinations, disorganized speech and disorganized behavior. Delusions are beliefs that are false.[1] Delusions may be plausible (such as thinking that one is being monitored by the FBI, or that a famous movie star is in love with oneself) or completely implausible (e.g., thinking that one's boss is actually an alien from another planet made to look like a human).

Hallucinations are perceptual phenomena, such as hearing, seeing, tasting, smelling or feeling something that is not actually

1. American Psychiatric Association, *Diagnostic and Statistical Manual*, 87–122.

present.[2] These are most frequently auditory, such as hearing derogatory voices, but can be very bizarre and unusual (e.g., feeling as if an alien is crawling under one's skin).

Disorganized speech is an abnormal thought process.[3] There are many types of disorganized speech. Often, people with disorganized speech jump quickly from one thought to another with little to no association between the two thoughts. Other times someone with disorganized speech may be thought blocking (when a person stops speaking suddenly due to loss of a thought) or have complete "word salad," in which there is no connection between the words being spoken.

Disorganized behavior is characterized by behavior that is inappropriate and gets in the way of normal functioning.[4] An example of bizarre behavior is purposeless behavior. For example, especially before the advent of psychiatric medications, patients would hold abnormal postures for hours at a time, such as standing on one leg, or holding one's arms out as if catching something, for no reason. Another example of disorganized behavior is very impulsive, disinhibited behavior, including impulsively assaulting people.

Negative symptoms are another type of psychotic symptom that are somewhat different than the four so-called "positive symptoms" described above. Negative symptoms involve a "loss" of functioning, such as anhedonia (the inability to experience pleasure), alogia (not talking), apathy, loss of motivation, loss of social interest, etc. People with substantial negative symptoms often appear flat, allow their level of hygiene to substantially deteriorate, and become isolated.

The quintessential serious mental illness is schizophrenia, and the very closely related schizoaffective disorder (for the purposes

2. American Psychiatric Association, *Diagnostic and Statistical Manual*, 87–122.

3. American Psychiatric Association, *Diagnostic and Statistical Manual*, 87–122.

4. American Psychiatric Association, *Diagnostic and Statistical Manual*, 87–122.

of this book, I will refer to both as schizophrenia given their similarities and that doing so will adequately address the theses and premises of this book). Schizophrenia is a chronic psychotic illness that usually begins in late adolescence or early adulthood.[5] Patients who develop schizophrenia often have a prodromal period that may last days to years, though usually six to twelve months. During the prodromal period, patients may experience attenuated delusions or hallucinations (i.e., delusions or hallucinations with less than 100 percent conviction) or milder forms of disorganized speech, disorganized behavior, and negative symptoms.[6] These patients are often teenagers who become withdrawn and demonstrate decreased performance at school. They also tend to isolate more from friends. They may experience varying degrees of depression and anxiety. While one may read this description of a prodromal person and think that it applies to a large number of otherwise "normal" teenagers, a person who is truly prodromal for schizophrenia will deteriorate rapidly into schizophrenia. That is, this is not a chronic or stable condition.

Schizophrenia is usually most active during the first ten years of the condition.[7] Patients typically require at least one hospitalization and experience relapsing and remitting symptoms during this time period. Schizophrenia, especially the positive symptoms, is quite responsive to antipsychotic medications, such as quetiapine, haloperidol, risperidone, olanzapine, and aripiprazole. Most people with schizophrenia require medication treatment for their entire lives. Unfortunately, the medications used to treat schizophrenia have substantial side effects. The older medications have side effects such as dystonia (severe muscle spasms) and dyskinesia (involuntary movements, such as what is experienced by people with Parkinson's disease). One previously common, but fortunately now much rarer, side effect of the older medications is tardive dyskinesia. Tardive dyskinesia is characterized by often permanent abnormal,

5. American Psychiatric Association, *Diagnostic and Statistical Manual*, 87–122.

6. Fusar-Poli et al., "Psychosis High-risk State," 107–20.

7. Lieberman, "First MB. Psychotic Disorders," 270–80.

jerky movements of the tongue, mouth, and potentially any part of the body. Needless to say, tardive dyskinesia is many times severely disabling and adds greatly to the stigma of schizophrenia. The newer medications have less motoric side effects, though are more associated with weight gain and increased cholesterol and triglycerides. Clozapine, which is, for reasons unknown to scientists even to this day, more effective than all other antipsychotic medications for treatment-resistant schizophrenia (and has saved many lives in this role),[8] causes the greatest amount of weight gain and requires weekly blood draws due to a rare, but potentially deadly, side effect called agranulocytosis (a severely low number of white blood cells, leaving one very vulnerable to infection).

After the first ten years of the illness, patients tend to have less acute episodes and less positive symptoms overall, though continue to have negative symptoms, as well as cognitive deficits (i.e., deficits in attention, concentration, memory, and other similar functions), that severely impair their functioning. These individuals usually still require medication management. While a small percentage of individuals with schizophrenia achieve a full remission, the majority of patients experience some, but not full, benefit from medications and are able to live relatively independently. A sizable minority are unresponsive to medications and require full-time care and chronic institutionalization. Many end up homeless or in the criminal justice system. The life expectancy for people with schizophrenia is substantially lower than it is for people without schizophrenia.[9]

Severe forms of bipolar disorder and major depressive disorder (heretofore referred to as depression) are also considered serious mental illness. In their most severe forms, both can include psychotic symptoms. Many people with bipolar disorder have psychotic symptoms.[10]

8. Kane et al., "Clozapine for the Treatment-Resistant Schizophrenic," 789–96.

9. Hjorthoj, "Years of Potential Life Lost," 295–301.

10. American Psychiatric Association, *Diagnostic and Statistical Manual*, 155–88.

Depression is characterized by sustained periods (i.e., at least two weeks) of low mood (although, ironically, a low mood is *not* a required criterion for the diagnosis of depression), low energy, anhedonia, impaired concentration, low self-esteem, impaired appetite, impaired sleep, slowing of speech and movements, and suicidal thoughts or behaviors.[11] These periods are episodic in nature, so that most people with depression have periods of weeks to months of depression followed by longer periods in between during which they are euthymic and have no depressive symptoms. In its most severe forms, depression can be associated with delusions or hallucinations and can be intractable and resistant to treatment.

Treatment for depression primarily consists of medications, such as fluoxetine, sertraline, and bupropion, as well as psychotherapy, or counseling.[12] The combination of medications and therapy works best. Severe forms of depression can be treated with electroconvulsive therapy (aka ECT or "shock" therapy) in which a very brief electrical pulse is applied to a person's temple causing a controlled and brief seizure. ECT techniques have been substantially refined over the years so that side effects, including memory loss, are now minimal. Many people receive ECT on an outpatient basis and even go to work after their ECT treatments. Depression is generally responsive to medication treatment. Many people with depression do not require lifelong treatment.

People with bipolar disorder generally have alternating episodes of depression and mania.[13] In between these episodes, they are often euthymic and have no symptoms of depression or mania. Mania is characterized by periods of at least a week of elevated or irritable mood, distractibility, impulsiveness, grandiosity, fast or pressured speech, racing thoughts, physical agitation, decreased need for sleep, or excess involvement in pleasurable activities. Psychotic symptoms in bipolar disorder often involve

11. American Psychiatric Association, *Diagnostic and Statistical Manual*, 155–88.

12. Mann, "Medical Management of Depression," 1819–34.

13. American Psychiatric Association, *Diagnostic and Statistical Manual*, 123–54.

themes related to their grandiosity, such as delusions of being a king or president, etc.

Lifelong treatment with medications is considered the standard of care for bipolar disorder. The medications used to treat bipolar disorder are similar to those for the treatment of schizophrenia. Other medications, called mood stabilizers, such as lithium and divalproex sodium, can also be used, as can antidepressants (paired with a mood stabilizer). ECT may be used in severe cases and can be effective. Patients with manic episodes often require hospitalization, as do patients with depressive episodes when one is feeling suicidal. Bipolar disorder tends to be responsive to medication treatment.

As described above, in very severe forms, bipolar disorder and depression can be intractable, resistant to medications, and manifest psychotic symptoms. These patients can appear similar to patients with schizophrenia. Sometimes, these patients can be so impaired that they become homeless.

With this brief introduction to serious mental illness, I will now delve into seven specific Bible passages which, I believe, either describe symptoms of serious mental illness in some form or, when examined from a psychiatrist's perspective, could reveal a great deal of information about the Biblical view of serious mental illness.

CHAPTER 3

Moses and the Consequence of Disobedience to God
(Deuteronomy 28)

In Deuteronomy 28, Moses describes to Israel the consequences of both obedience and disobedience to God's laws. In the first half of the chapter he describes the blessings of obedience, described in terms of child-bearing, agriculture, military and political success, and general prosperity as God's people. In the latter and larger part of the chapter, Moses describes what would happen to Israel if they were not obedient to God's commandments. He first clearly addresses the opposite of what he described in the first part of the chapter—namely, that "The fruit of your womb will be cursed, and the crops of your land, and the calves of your herds and the lambs of your flocks" (v. 18). Moses goes on to describe even greater and worse consequences of disobedience, including "confusion . . . until you are destroyed and come to sudden ruin because of the evil you have done in forsaking him" (v. 20) as well as with "diseases until he has destroyed you from the land you are entering to possess" (v. 21). After describing more political defeat, Moses returns to the medical theme, telling Israel that disobedience with God's laws will result in "the boils of Egypt and with tumors, festering sores and the itch, from which you cannot be cured. The Lord will afflict you with madness, blindness and confusion of mind. . . . The sights you see will drive you mad" (vv. 27–28, 34). (Of note, such references were used throughout the Old Testament; for example, ""I will send my terror ahead of you and throw into confusion every nation you encounter. I will make all your enemies turn their backs and run" [Exod 23:27]; "'On that day I will strike every horse with panic and its rider with madness,' declares the Lord" [Zech 12:4]. For this chapter, I will focus on Deuteronomy 28, and similar points could be made about these additional passages.)

Moses continues this description of complete tragedy and failure, describing a situation in which Israel is sold as slaves, families are broken up, and there is economic collapse, as well as complete and total suffering and hardship in foreign lands. To confirm how desolate these consequences would be, Moses describes how the Israelites would feel were all of these calamities to occur, "There the Lord will give you an anxious mind, eyes weary with longing, and a despairing heart" (v. 65).

Moses was a very effective leader and orator, capable of leading a whole nation through pivotal and severe transitions over many of their most formative decades. Further, he led Israel nearly a millennium before science, medicine, and even literacy were commonplace in general society. Therefore, in order to be effective in his description of the consequences of not following God's laws, Moses had to use obvious, real, and tangible examples of these consequences, rather than obscure, abstract, or metaphorical concepts. Therefore, he described slavery, infertility, drought, pestilence, political conquest, and disease, all things that the Israelites would have been expected to understand. Similarly, in his descriptions of "confusion," "anxious mind," and "madness," Moses is not describing the spiritual, internal suffering that comes with not following God's laws. This would have been irrelevant, misunderstood, and inconsistent with Moses's themes. Rather, he is more likely describing untreated mental illness, including psychosis and mania. For Moses to describe these psychiatric conditions along-side many other severe and well-understood tragedies, physical illnesses, and hardships suggests that they must have been so prevalent, devastating, and common that they would have been understood by the common Israelite. Further, although Moses gave few details about how "confusion" and "madness" manifest, as opposed to later descriptions of psychiatric illness in the Bible, it would be reasonable to assume that just using this language would elicit a clear understanding from the Israelites, even though different language is used today.

CHAPTER 4

King Saul's Psychotic Depression
(1 Samuel 15–31)

In 1 Samuel 15, King Saul disobeyed God when he spared King Agag of the Amalekites and their best livestock from death, after being explicitly told by God to destroy all of the Amalekites, including the livestock. Samuel then told Saul that because of his disobedience, "the Lord has rejected you as king over Israel!" (v. 26). Saul became very depressed and pleaded to be allowed to remain the king of Israel. The next several chapters describe the extent of King Saul's descent into depression in greater detail, as well as his development of paranoia.

After living a somewhat privileged life, Saul, described in 1 Samuel 9:2 as being "as handsome a young man as could be found anywhere in Israel, and he was a head taller than anyone else," experienced a severe stressor—namely, the loss of his rule over Israel—and developed a severe depression. In the first part of 1 Samuel 16, the authors describe how David was appointed by Samuel as the next king of Israel, and in verses 14–23, the authors describe how Saul became depressed and required the soothing of David's music to, at least temporarily, feel better. In keeping with the understanding of mental illness at this time in history as being caused by demons or spirits, Saul's depression was described by the authors in verse 14 by saying that "Now the Spirit of the Lord had departed from Saul, and an evil spirit from the Lord tormented him," and in verse 23, describing Saul's response to David's music, "Then relief would come to Saul; he would feel better, and the evil spirit would leave him." Because of the effects of David's music on King Saul, he held David in high regard and kept him in his service.

King Saul's affection for David quickly turned to jealousy, and then outright paranoia, after David killed Goliath, became great friends with Saul's son Jonathan, and began to receive adulation and adoration from the Israelites for his growing and numerous accomplishments. In 1 Samuel 18, the authors describe Saul's growing paranoia, again in keeping with the understanding at this time in history that mental illness was caused by spirits and demons, "The next day an evil spirit from God came forcefully on Saul" (v. 10; of note, that the description of this "evil spirit" was only consistent with figurative language from an ancient, pre-Enlightenment narrative that did not understand mental illness rather than reality is suggested by the realization that no evil spirits could come from God; by definition, Satan is the source of all evil; this will be discussed in greater detail in later chapters). Saul's paranoia became so great that he tried to kill David on numerous occasions. Not only did Saul try to kill David himself, he developed schemes by which David would be killed by others, including to have David marry his daughters, thereby becoming an enemy of the Philistines and a leader of Saul's armies, which would in turn lead to him becoming targeted by the Philistines. Of course, none of these attempts worked, despite the number of them. In fact, David became even more successful and adored, to the point that Saul's daughter Michal, whom David married, and Saul's son Jonathan, protected David, to Saul's great dismay.

This only served to increase Saul's paranoia. In 1 Samuel 20, after realizing that his son Jonathan was protecting David, Saul tried to kill his own son. In 1 Samuel 22, after finding out that the priests of Nob helped David (as described in chapter 5 of this book), he incorporated the priests of Nob into his delusion and decided to kill them. The exchange between Saul and Ahimelek the priest very accurately illustrates the extent of Saul's delusion. In verse 13, Saul says to Ahimelek, "Why have you conspired against me, you and the son of Jesse, giving him bread and a sword and inquiring of God for him, so that he has rebelled against me and lies in wait for me, as he does today?" Here, Saul accused David of persecuting him and Ahimelek of conspiring with him, when in fact it was the reverse; Saul was persecuting David. This manner of thinking, in which Saul denied his own impulse and rather attributed it to someone else, is quite typical for people who are paranoid and have persecutory delusions. This is referred to as projection (this "defense mechanism," as it is called, is commonly observed in, though not exclusive to, delusions of persecution). However, in practice, to the layperson, or even to a beginning clinician, dealing with a paranoid person can be very difficult because, in the absence of other symptoms, that person may seem completely plausible, leaving the observer very confused as to what to believe, rather than immediately recognizing that the person has a mental illness. This was illustrated by Ahimelek's response to Saul

> Who of all your servants is as loyal as David, the king's son-in-law, captain of your bodyguard and highly respected in your household? Was that day the first time I inquired of God for him? Of course not! Let not the king accuse your servant or any of his father's family, for your servant knows nothing at all about this whole affair. (vv. 14–15)

In as clear a demonstration of Saul's paranoia as anything, he was fully convinced that David was persecuting him and that Ahimelek was helping him, and so ordered the priests of Nob to be killed. However, even Saul's own guard were unwilling to kill the priests because of how baseless the claims were, so Saul had Doeg the Edomite kill them.

Saul's delusion was all consuming. He continued to pursue David. Even after David spared Saul's life in the desert of En Gedi,

Saul continued to pursue him, even after promising to no longer pursue him, until David again spared Saul's life in the desert of Ziph. Saul was eventually killed in battle (or more specifically killed himself).

This story of King Saul from when he was told that he would be removed as King of Israel to his development of depression and descent into what appears to have been severe and unrelenting paranoia is a lesson in psychotic depression and in particular the role of stress in mental illness. As is often the case with mental illness, the severe psychosocial stress of being removed from power appears to have triggered King Saul's depression. Episodes of mental illness often follow, or are exacerbated by, some type of stress, which can include, but is not limited to, medical illness, drug use, relationship/work/financial/family problems, or even puberty, which is a very significant stressor. Further, in psychological terms, "good" (e.g., getting married) or "bad" (e.g., death of a loved one) events can be equally stressful and therefore can both precede an episode of mental illness. Some of these stressors are modifiable or avoidable, such as drug use, while others are not, such as puberty. Probably more than anything else, that a patient's condition follows some type of stress is cited by many patients as a reason for why they do not have a "real" mental illness, but rather really just have a condition related to stress which, in their minds, does not require medication treatment. Besides this being a fallacious argument, it is also incorrect. Stressful experiences are unavoidable. It is never a matter of if, but when, a person will have a stressor, and how frequently. There is not a single person on Earth who does not experience stressful, and sometimes tragic, experiences on a regular basis. That is simply life. Theoretically, if one were to never have stressful experiences then there would most likely be much less mental illness, but that would also be incompatible with life as we experience it. Certainly, less drug use, better relationships, and overall healthier living would substantially decrease the incidence of mental illness. However, they would by no means eradicate it. Saying that a mental illness only came on because of stress is somewhat similar to saying that one is hungry only because they have not eaten in several hours. There are many ways to minimize the feeling of hunger, including scheduling meals more frequently, eating a similar amount at every meal, etc., but ultimately hunger will set in because eating is a part of life. There is almost no practical way to avoid it. In other words, whether or not a psychiatric episode follows a stressful event does not generally affect how we think about this person's mental illness (except in more mild circumstances when a diagnosis of an adjustment disorder is given)[1] and definitely does not invalidate it or suggest that a condition is something besides mental illness. Based on current knowledge (though hopefully this will soon change), given that stressful events are an inherent part of a person's life, a person with a predisposition for anxiety, depression, psychosis, or another mental illness will likely develop that condition without an intervention. Unfortunately, the fallacious argument that an episode of depression, anxiety, psychosis, or something else that follows a stressful event is any less valid than an episode that does not follow a stressful event is probably the number one argument given to me by my patients for why they do not need, or should not take, medications.

The story of King Saul also highlights the severe condition of psychotic depression. Depression itself is a common psychiatric condition, affecting many people at some time in their lives.[2] In a very severe form, depression can include psychotic symptoms, especially delusions or hallucinations, that may be mood congruent, meaning the psychotic symptoms are consistent with other themes of one's illness (e.g., nihilistic delusions in depression), or mood incongruent, meaning the psychotic symptoms are inconsistent with other themes of one's illness, such as a voice or hallucination telling someone that he or she is God when one is very depressed. King Saul's persecutory delusion was mood congruent as his depression and feelings of loss and destruction were consistent with his delusions of persecution from David and others.

1. American Psychiatric Association, *Diagnostic and Statistical Manual*, 265–90.

2. American Psychiatric Association, *Diagnostic and Statistical Manual*, 155–88.

As mentioned above, delusions that occur in the context of depression can be very difficult to identify or understand, as opposed to others experienced by people with schizophrenia. The reason is that while people with schizophrenia often appear very bizarre, disheveled, and have numerous other symptoms (such as hallucinations, disorganization, etc. as described in chapter 2), individuals with depression and a delusion may have less bizarre delusions and appear to be completely believable. For example, they may be delusional about something that is possible or plausible, such as being persecuted by someone, rather than something that is impossible, such as communicating with aliens. Compounding this is that while depression without psychosis is quite responsive to medications, and even without medications episodes of depression may resolve within months, depression with psychosis is less responsive to medications and more likely to persist,[3] as in the case of King Saul's condition. In general, among all psychiatric conditions, the development of psychotic symptoms implies a more fulminant, severe, and potentially refractory condition. Such was the case in the story of King Saul, whose psychotic depression may have lasted until his death.

3. Keller et al., "Current Issues," 877–85.

CHAPTER 5

King David Feigns Psychosis
(1 Samuel 21)

---

1 Samuel 21 describes some of David's journeys while fleeing King Saul, who wanted to kill him. David had just been warned by Jonathan, King Saul's son, that King Saul wanted to kill him. This was done at no small risk to Jonathan as clearly indicated in 1 Samuel 20 in which Saul, after finding out that Jonathan had warned David that he wanted to kill him, almost killed his own son Jonathan.

After a short stop at Nob, likely to receive provisions or emotional support, David proceeded to Gath, in Philistia, for protection. David did so at great risk, given that he was an enemy of the Philistines and had killed one of their greatest warriors, Goliath. Presumably, David went with Goliath's sword, given to him by Ahimelek the priest, as he thought that possessing the sword would provide some amount of protection.

Although it appears that King Achish of Gath did allow for David's protection, one can gather from the passage that David remained extremely fearful for his life, which is understandable being in enemy territory and being sought after by Saul. There was no guarantee that King Achish nor anyone else would not betray him by killing him themselves or turning him over to King Saul. Therefore, out of desperation, and in order to elicit feelings of pity and sympathy, David pretended to be psychotic, "So he pretended to be insane in their presence; and while he was in their hands he acted like a madman, making marks on the doors of the gate and letting saliva run down his beard" (v. 13). As obvious a ploy as this may seem to the reader, it appears to have had the desired effect on King Achish, as described in the following two verses: "Achish said to his servants, 'Look at the man! He is insane! Why bring him to me? Am I so short of madmen that you have to bring this fellow here to carry on like this in front of me? Must this man come into my house?'" (vv. 14–15). (Of note, there are other times in the Bible when references are made to a person accusing another of being insane. For example: "At this point Festus interrupted Paul's defense. 'You are out of your mind, Paul!' he shouted. 'Your great learning is driving you insane.' 'I am not insane, most excellent Festus,' Paul replied. 'What I am saying is true and reasonable'" (Acts 26:24–25). For this chapter, I will focus on 1 Samuel 21, and similar points could be made about these additional passages.)

That David used the tactic of acting psychotic, and that King Achish and his group so readily recognized this behavior, suggests the relative commonality of this behavior and a general understanding of the presence of psychosis, even if such individuals were perceived as a bother and little could be done. Further, some may suggest that "letting saliva run down his beard" (v. 13) is more typical of a seizure. However, the context in which this happened, for example "making marks on the doors of the gate" (v. 13), which is not behavior that would be typically observed during a full tonic-clonic seizure, suggests otherwise. Rather, this level of disorganization is common in serious mental illness, such as schizophrenia or bipolar disorder. When untreated, patients often act in a very disorganized manner, preoccupied by auditory hallucinations. I frequently walk through the waiting room in my clinic or through the inpatient unit at my hospital and find my sicker patients writing nonsensical material on furniture or the walls. Further, it is the case that in modern times drooling is observed primarily as a side effect of the medications used to treat psychotic disorders. However, before the advent of psychotropic medications in the early 1950s, motoric abnormalities and catatonia, which may involve maintaining awkward and unnatural positions, such as holding one's mouth open, for hours to days at a time, were commonplace. Together, this information suggests that David very accurately mimicked psychosis, and that this behavior was widely understood.

Finally, King Achish's response to David's feigned psychosis ("Look at the man! He is insane! Why bring him to me? Am I so short of madmen that you have to bring this fellow here to carry on like this in front of me? Must this man come into my house?" [v. 14–15]) is remarkably similar to how many individuals, even today, three millennia after David's time, respond to being confronted by psychotic individuals. Namely, like King Achish, many people still consider individuals with mental illness to be a burden and are annoyed at their presence. The unfortunate and completely inaccurate implication of this type of response to mental illness is that serious mental illness is more within one's control than it is "biological" and out of one's control. Could one imagine someone responding to a person with other medical conditions, such as a heart attacks, strokes, or pneumonia, in this way? This generally does not happen because although each of these conditions can result in substantial disability, cost, and imposition on someone else's life (e.g., a family member or caregiver), people generally understand that these conditions are beyond one's control. However, although psychiatric conditions such as schizophrenia and bipolar disorder are almost completely "biological" and a result of mostly unmodifiable risk factors (e.g., at the current time, there is essentially no way to prevent schizophrenia or bipolar disorder, while conditions such as diabetes, heart attacks, and strokes have genetic components but are in large part preventable by modifying behaviors such as diet, exercise, and smoking), many people still regard even major mental disorders primarily as a result of bad parenting or moral weakness. Although some progress has been made, huge proportions of society, including religious individuals, remain misinformed about mental illness and treat individuals with mental illness with disdain and disgrace. Therefore, this story of David and King Achish not only enlightens us about the presence of mental illness in Biblical times, but also emphasizes the timelessness of stigma.

CHAPTER 6

Jonah's Narcissism
and Severe Depression
(Jonah 4)

Jonah was an Old Testament prophet who was told by God in Jonah 1 to go to Nineveh and preach to them about their disobedience to God. At this point it is unclear why Jonah did not want to go to Nineveh, but he did not and tried to escape God by going to Tarshish. On the way, God sent a storm that almost capsized the boat on which Jonah was traveling. The boat was saved only when the sailors threw Jonah overboard. Jonah was then swallowed by a large fish, and after three days and nights of repentance and prayer, was released (Jonah 2).

In Jonah 3, God again commanded Jonah to go to Nineveh and preach to them about their disobedience to God and that they would be overthrown after forty days. The king and subjects of Nineveh repented, and God spared them from destruction.

Jonah 4 is a remarkable ending to the story of Jonah. In Jonah 4, Jonah argues with God and basically tells God that he knew better than he did:

But to Jonah this seemed very wrong, and he became angry. He prayed to the Lord, "Isn't this what I said, Lord, when I was still at home? That is what I tried to forestall by fleeing to Tarshish. I knew that you are a gracious and compassionate God, slow to anger and abounding in love, a God who relents from sending calamity. Now, Lord, take away my life, for it is better for me to die than to live." (vv. 1–3)

After seeing that Nineveh was saved, Jonah became very angry at God for wasting his time, in Jonah's mind. He basically told God that he knew that God would save the Ninevites, and so felt that it was a waste of time for him to go to them. In fact, Jonah became so upset that he asked God to take his life as he felt that he no longer had a reason to live.

One does not have to be a psychiatrist to immediately recognize the grandiosity, hubris, and narcissism that would be required for Jonah to question God in such a manner. And Jonah was not a nonbeliever, uneducated, or ignorant. Rather, he was one of God's chosen prophets. Yet, despite fully understanding who God is, he felt that he knew more than God. This is an incredible description of narcissism, foremost demonstrated by Jonah's hypertrophied sense of arrogance and haughtiness that is typical of such people.

In verse 4, God attempts to correct Jonah's terrible misconceptions, "But the Lord replied, 'Is it right for you to be angry?'" However, it appears that this had little effect on Jonah. Therefore, God, out of his great love for Jonah, continued to try to help Jonah understand the error of his thinking by putting him in an analogous situation. Namely, he allowed a large plant to provide shade for Jonah. He then sent a worm to eat the plant, which left Jonah exposed to the very hot and uncomfortable conditions. Jonah again became angry and asked to die. God once again asked Jonah if it were right for him to be so angry, to which Jonah replied, "'It is,' he said. 'And I'm so angry I wish I were dead'" (v. 9). It may seem obvious to the reader that Jonah's behavior had substantially regressed to the point of being immature and fickle, and it was. God used this opportunity to continue his lesson to Jonah. Namely, God made the observation to Jonah that he was initially so appreciative of the plant when it was providing him shade, and then became so angry once it had withered, not because of the plant itself, but for selfish reasons—namely, because it was no longer providing him shade. God then explained to Jonah that besides being extremely selfish, how would he think that God would feel about trying to save 120,000 people?

Once again, this passage provides a textbook example of narcissism. Besides the arrogance and haughtiness of individuals with narcissism, narcissists display several other traits. They are exploitative of others, entitled, and lack empathy. Jonah demonstrates all of these character traits during this passage. Jonah did not seem to care at all about the plant or the Ninevites. In both circumstances, he cared only about his own comfort and desires, regardless of what happened to Nineveh or the plant. Jonah did not want to be inconvenienced by traveling to Nineveh and preaching to them, even if that could have saved 120,000 lives. He cared more about not traveling. Further, Jonah did not care about the plant and whether it lived or died. He cared only about whether he was comfortable and had shade.

Individuals with narcissism also tend to have very unstable, quickly changing, and overly dramatic moods, as clearly demonstrated by Jonah. Within hours, Jonah went from feeling happy and content, to begging God to take his life. As described above, one would expect this behavior from young children, but not from an adult. However, this type of labile, unstable, fickle affect is typical of individuals with narcissism. There was no reason for Jonah to want to die. He was simply uncomfortable, inconvenienced, or unhappy. An adult with a more stable, healthy set of emotions would have been appropriately upset and uncomfortable given these circumstances, but would not have asked to die.

This behavior is very typical of individuals with narcissism, or more specifically narcissistic personality disorder.[1] The personality

---

1. American Psychiatric Association, *Diagnostic and Statistical Manual*, 645–84.

disorders are a group of psychiatric conditions that are considered characterological, in that they are chronic, begin in adolescence or early adulthood, and are pervasive. People afflicted with these disorders usually have very little insight into them, which cause substantial social and occupational dysfunction. These conditions are very common, and it is likely that most readers of this book know of numerous examples among their family, friends, or coworkers and acquaintances. Jonah was a classic example of a narcissist. The Bible is not clear about whether Jonah was able to change. Fortunately, though medication-based treatments are somewhat limited and primarily focused on treating concomitant symptoms, such as anxiety and depression, these individuals tend to be most amenable to psychodynamic or psychoanalytic therapies (i.e., Freudian-type therapy), as well as more structured psychotherapies that target the labile affect and maladaptive behaviors, such as dialectical behavior therapy (DBT).

In Jonah's case, it appears that his narcissism may have been complicated by the development of a severe depression. Jonah's depression is most clearly manifest by his repeated desire to die, as well as his unhappy mood. Very little is known about Jonah's earlier or later life. Therefore, it is difficult to say whether his depression was longstanding and chronic or primarily related to his narcissism. However, in psychodynamic terms, considering only the information at hand, we would say that Jonah developed a depression as a result of a "narcissistic injury." A narcissistic injury is when a narcissist experiences a threat to one's inflated and oversized sense of oneself. The effect is often intense and can manifest as depression, aggression, violence, or other extreme, maladaptive behavior aimed at displacing one's negative emotions (e.g., drug use). By definition, a narcissist has emotional instability. Therefore, instead of appropriately dealing with being corrected by God, Jonah overreacted to God's response and directed his anger, confusion and helplessness inward. His internalized feelings conflicted with his fragile sense of narcissism and grandiosity, leading to further despair, feelings of inadequacy, and ultimately a desire to die. These sorts of responses are not uncommon in general clinical practice and are, at least partly, amenable to treatment. However, a substantial minority of these individuals do end up killing themselves as their narcissistic injury and resultant depression are too much for them to bear. Ultimately, we do not know what happened to Jonah. However, examining his story through the lens of serious mental illness reveals that serious mental illness could affect anybody, even one of the greatest of the Old Testament prophets. No one is immune to mental illness and the ravages thereof.

There are numerous other examples of major Old Testament figures who experienced great despair and symptoms suggestive of depression, albeit many in the face of mourning or severe stressors. Naomi, the great great grandmother of King David, lost her husband and both of her sons to a severe famine in Moab (Ruth 1). When she heard about the relative abundance of food in her hometown of Bethlehem, she went to Bethlehem accompanied by her daughter-in-law Ruth. When Naomi arrived in Bethlehem, she was recognized by the townspeople who asked if she was in fact Naomi, to which Naomi replied, "'Don't call me Naomi,' she told them. 'Call me Mara, because the Almighty has made my life very bitter. I went away full, but the Lord has brought me back empty. Why call me Naomi? The Lord has afflicted me; the Almighty has brought misfortune upon me'" (vv. 20–21).

Job, in the context of losing his family, possessions, and health, to the point of having severe skin sores and living in destitution, also became extremely depressed. In Job 6:8–9 he expresses his severe depression, and, like Jonah, asked God to take his life: "Oh, that I might have my request, that God would grant what I hope for, that God would be willing to crush me, to let loose his hand and cut off my life!"

The great prophet Elijah also asked for God to take his life. During the reign of King Ahab, there was waning support for the true God of Israel and increased support for false gods such as Baal (1 Kings 18). Much of this support came from the influence of King Ahab's wife, Jezebel, on policy in Israel. In an attempt to prove once and for all that the Lord is God, Elijah challenged the approximately 850 false prophets to have their gods set fire to a bull on a table on Mount Carmel. After hours of praying, dancing, and chanting, the false prophets were unable to have their gods set the bull on fire. Elijah then put his bull on an altar and drenched it, the table, and a surrounding trench with twelve jars of water. He prayed to God and the bull and everything around it were consumed with fire. Elijah then had all of the false prophets killed. This severely angered Jezebel, who sent word to Elijah that she was going to kill him (1 Kings 19). Elijah became very scared, depressed, and ran away. Elijah became so distraught that he asked God to take his life:

> Elijah was afraid and ran for his life. When he came to Beersheba in Judah, he left his servant there, while he himself went a day's journey into the wilderness. He came to a broom bush, sat down under it and prayed that he might die. "I have had enough, Lord," he said. "Take my life; I am no better than my ancestors." Then he lay down under the bush and fell asleep. (vv. 3–5).

Jeremiah the prophet, who foretold and warned Israel about their destruction and capture, also asked God to take his life. In Jeremiah 20, after a priest named Pashhur had Jeremiah beaten and placed in the stocks for his prophesies, Jeremiah said,

> Cursed be the day I was born! May the day my mother bore me not be blessed! Cursed be the man who brought my father the news, who made him very glad, saying, "A child is born to you—a son!" May that man be like the towns the Lord overthrew without pity. May he hear wailing in the morning, a battle cry at noon. For he did not kill me in the womb, with my mother as my grave, her womb enlarged forever. Why did I ever come out of the womb to see trouble and sorrow and to end my days in shame? (vv. 14–18)

Finally, Moses asked God to take his life in Numbers 11. After leaving Egypt and while wandering in the wilderness, the Israelites often complained about their limited food supplies and relative hardships. As the leader, Moses took on much of the burdens and responsibilities of the Israelites, so much so that he became over-whelmed and asked God to take his life, "He asked the Lord:

> Why have you brought this trouble on your servant? What have I done to displease you that you put the burden of all these people on me? Did I conceive all these people? Did I give them birth? Why do you tell me to carry them in my arms, as a nurse carries an infant, to the land you promised on oath to their ancestors? Where can I get meat for all these people? They keep wailing to me, "Give us meat to eat!" I cannot carry all these people by myself; the burden is too heavy for me. If this is how you are going to treat me, please go ahead and kill me—if I have found favor in your eyes—and do not let me face my own ruin. (vv. 11–15)

God eased Moses's burden by instructing him to identify seventy elders who could share the burden and leadership responsibilities.

The stories of Jonah, Moses, Jeremiah, Elijah, Job, and Naomi highlight that symptoms of severe depression and suicidal thoughts were common in Old Testament times and among the greatest and most revered prophets and people of all time.

CHAPTER 7

Nebuchadnezzar's Psychotic Break and Redemption
(Daniel 4)

Daniel 4 tells the story of Nebuchadnezzar, by Nebuchadnezzar, presumably inserted into the book of Daniel by himself to provide additional meaning to the story. This chapter starts with a description of Nebuchadnezzar's dream, is followed by the interpretation of the dream, and ends with the fulfillment of the dream and the aftermath.

Nebuchadnezzar tells Daniel (also referred to as Belteshazzar) that he dreamt of a spectacular tree that provided food and shelter to a great number of birds and animals. After the initial description, Nebuchadnezzar describes a "loud voice" from heaven stating that the tree should be stripped bare so that only "the stump and its roots" remain (vv. 14–15). The voice went on to say, "Let him be drenched with the dew of heaven, and let him live with the animals among the plants of the earth. Let his mind be changed from that of a man and let him be given the mind of an animal, till seven times pass by for him" (vv. 15–16).

No one in Nebuchadnezzar's kingdom was able to interpret this dream, so Nebuchadnezzar asked for Daniel's help. Daniel relatively quickly understood the dream and was "terrified" about sharing his interpretation to Nebuchadnezzar (v. 19). With Nebuchadnezzar's encouragement and assurance, Daniel explained that the tree was Nebuchadnezzar and his kingdom, and that if he were to not repent and acknowledge the power and omnipotence of God, he would not only lose his kingdom but be forced to live among lowly animals (i.e., as opposed to among animals at the top of the food chain or of a more splendid nature, such as lions or eagles) for seven years before his kingdom would be restored to him.

Nebuchadnezzar apparently did not accept or believe this interpretation. Twelve months later, after praising himself for the richness and glory of Babylon, he was removed from power and began living among animals, eating grass to survive, and was unable to clean himself (i.e., "his hair grew like the feathers of an eagle and his nails like the claws of a bird" [v. 33]).

What Nebuchadnezzar experienced sounds very much like a psychotic break, consistent with the development of an untreated serious mental illness, such as schizophrenia, or severe forms of depression or bipolar disorder that are unrelenting and have many of the same psychotic signs and symptoms as does schizophrenia. While Nebuchadnezzar's use of the word "sanity" (v. 34) clearly implies that he developed such a condition, there are numerous other pieces of evidence that suggest this. Namely, that Nebuchadnezzar was forced to live outside, without shelter, and among animals, suggests a severe level of disorganized thought and behavior, typical of people with untreated psychosis, that precluded an ability to interact with normal society. This is reinforced by his inability for, or disinterest in, normal hygiene. This passage also correctly highlights that mental illness often tends to afflict people abruptly and when they are at the height of their physical and mental capabilities. Further, mental illness does not discriminate between ages, races, cultures, or income level. My clinic is replete with individuals who have no money or are millionaires, who have

Ivy League educations or limited education, of any race and culture, who are religious and not religious, working as professionals (such as physicians) or as unskilled workers, etc. No one, not even the king of Babylon, is immune to mental illness.

While reading this passage one might think that this account of psychosis seems exaggerated, overly dramatic, or not consistent with current psychiatric phenomenology. This would be a natural but incorrect assumption. Unfortunately, this presentation is actually very typical of many psychotic patients, even in modern times. For example, although the majority of people with psychotic disorders do substantially improve on medications, a large minority do not. In addition, many individuals with psychotic disorders do not have adequate insight into their condition to accept treatment, and therefore remain unmedicated. Unfortunately, in many cases, these individuals end up exactly like Nebuchadnezzar—they shun society or help of any sort, and often refuse to live with, or receive the assistance of, very supportive and willing family members, friends, or social services (such as shelters). They often appear very disorganized and disheveled, have long and uncut head and facial hair, have long nails from a lack of grooming, and are heavily soiled. Their speech is often disorganized, sometimes to the point of being completely incomprehensible (technically referred to as "word salad"). These individuals may prefer to live alone, on the streets (in urban areas) or in wooded areas (in rural areas), isolated from society. Many of these individuals comprise the homeless populations that are seen every day, but otherwise are not paid attention.

While this presentation does represent a more severe form of psychosis, it is not uncommon. Fortunately, most of these individuals are still at least partially responsive to medications. However, in Nebuchadnezzar's time, there were no medications capable of treating psychosis, so seven years of such severe symptoms would not only have been possible, but likely. In fact, it is most likely that this description of his behavior and appearance for those seven years was quite typical of people with psychotic illness in historical times. It is probable that Nebuchadnezzar was one of many people with untreated serious mental illness living among the plants and animals in the wilderness around Babylon and in Mesopotamia.

Nebuchadnezzar then shares that it was only after fully acknowledging God's greatness and power that his "sanity was restored" (v. 34), and he once again became the ruler of Babylon. There is another very important lesson to be had from the story of Nebuchadnezzar. As told by Nebuchadnezzar, all he had to do to return to his previous mental state was to accept the power and glory of God, which he did, after seven years, and which was a miracle. Of note, that Nebuchadnezzar was healed so abruptly and miraculously is often provided by religious individuals, who do not believe in psychiatric illnesses as true medical conditions, as proof that Nebuchadnezzar's condition was not psychiatric in nature and that psychiatric medications are similarly invalid. These individuals also often believe that psychiatric illness is primarily a moral condition and that the answer to treating their condition is to wait for a miracle or sign from God, rather than to see a psychiatrist, take a medication, or admit themselves into a psychiatric hospital. I have engaged in hundreds of hours of discussions with individuals with these beliefs, trying to help them understand that their situations, or those of their loved ones, are very similar to Nebuchadnezzar's. I would submit that psychiatric treatment and medications are, in many cases, no less miraculous than God's will. I have treated hundreds of patients who have appeared very similar to Nebuchadnezzar—refusing medications for years, homeless, in extreme poverty, disheveled, and completely asocial—become essentially completely normal, functioning human beings after accepting, or sometimes being forced by the court system to take, psychiatric medications. Often, it takes seven or more years for a person to develop enough insight to realize that they have a psychiatric condition and that psychiatric medications can be the vessels of change. But if psychiatric medications were not available in Nebuchadnezzar's time, how could his recovery be viewed as anything but a miracle? In addition to the possibilities that Nebuchadnezzar's illness had simply run its course (seen in a minority of patients), or that God simply cured Nebuchadnezzar's mental illness (which remains very possible), there remain other potential explanations for Nebuchadnezzar's recovery that are fully consistent with the Scripture as well as with psychiatry. For example, the first antipsychotic medication ever developed for medical use was developed in the mid-twentieth century.[1] Reserpine, which has antipsychotic properties, was developed around the same time. The plant from which reserpine was isolated, Rauwolfia serpentina (Indian snakeroot), had been used in the Indian subcontinent and Asia as a treatment for insanity for centuries before being used by Western medicine. It is possible that Nebuchadnezzar's recovery was due to coming into contact with Rauwolfia serpentine.

This possibility leads to another interpretation of Nebuchadnezzar's recovery which would support the thesis of this book, and, to me, in no way diminish the Biblical impact of the story of Nebuchadnezzar. Fundamental to this story is that Nebuchadnezzar was able to change his whole philosophy and worldview. The miracle of Nebuchadnezzar is not that he became psychotic and then recovered—as described above and throughout this book, even serious mental illness is often treatable—this happens every day. The miracle is that Nebuchadnezzar became a believer. He initially gave no glory to God, but rather genuinely believed that he was responsible for the greatness and majesty of the kingdom of Babylon. As in Colossians 1:16, "For in Him all things were created: things in heaven and on earth, visible and invisible, whether thrones or powers or rulers or authorities; all things were created through him and for him"; or John 1:3, "Through him all things were made; without him nothing was made that has been made." God is omnipotent and the Creator of everything. The perspective that God is the Creator of everything and that all good things happen through God is a fundamental belief of Judeo-Christianity and was completely unappreciated by Nebuchadnezzar. As described numerous times throughout the Bible, we are not to be concerned with material or earthly things for their own value, but rather in how they may enhance our salvation and relationship with God.

1. Lehmann and Ban, "History of the Psychopharmacology of Schizophrenia," 152–62.

The miracle of the story of King Nebuchadnezzar was not that he was healed of a serious mental illness, but that he learned to accept God's role in his life and realized salvation.

CHAPTER 8

The Miracle
of the (Gadarene) Demoniac
(Luke 8, Mark 5, Matthew 8)

In one of the most well-known stories of the New Testament, told in all three Synoptic Gospels, Jesus had just stepped ashore along the Sea of Galilee when he was met by one or two "demon-possessed" men (v. 27). (In Luke and Mark, he heals one man. In Matthew he heals two men. Henceforth, I will use Luke 8 as the primary source for this account and will refer to one man, although the discussion and points do not change whether there were one or two men.) Examining this story from the perspective of serious mental illness could provide a great deal of understanding about serious mental illness. As stated above, it is important to iterate that my goal in this chapter is not to change the readers' view that the miracle of the (Gadarene) demoniac is about serious mental illness per se, but rather to use this great miracle to enhance what we understand about serious mental illness by examining it from a post-Enlightenment perspective. I will undertake to do so now.

According to the Gospels, the man was disheveled and "had not worn clothes or lived in a house, but had lived in the tombs" (v. 27). It is possible that this "demon-possessed" man was also suffering from an untreated serious mental illness, such as schizophrenia or a severe form of bipolar disorder. In this context, this story underscores the clear pattern in which individuals in the Bible with symptoms of serious mental illness are disheveled, transient/homeless, and live away from society, similar to the story of Nebuchadnezzar in Daniel 4. As mentioned previously, this type of behavior, namely inattention to hygiene, as well as chosen homelessness, are very unfortunate traits of especially untreated serious mental illness.

The Gospels go on to describe the man as being hyperactive and disorganized, so much so that he had "broken his chains and had been driven by the demon into the solitary places" (v. 29). These behaviors are unfortunately very typical of untreated severe and acute mental illness. For example, when patients with severe manic or psychotic episodes are in the emergency room, they frequently become severely agitated, loud, and hyperactive, to the point that they become unable to control themselves. They often have persecutory delusions, such as that people in the emergency room or elsewhere want to kill them, or that devils or other spirits are trying to control them. They may also experience auditory hallucinations that seem very real to them and command them to kill themselves or other people. In these cases, patients will sometimes try to harm or kill themselves or someone else, in order to protect themselves. These situations are considered among the most dangerous and acute in psychiatry and require emergency and extreme management. The first step in the management of such situations would be for these patients to be offered medications that they can choose to take by mouth. If they refuse to do so, which is often the case due to their agitation, disorganization, and impaired insight, and if they are still severely agitated and dangerous, approximately five or six very large, football lineman-sized security guards will hold the patient down (one for each limb and one for the head, at the minimum) for an injection of medication.

The striking reality is that, while in a state of agitation and untreated severe psychosis, many times compounded by illicit substance use, people lose their inhibitions and become inordinately strong, so that even smaller people, men or women, become so enormously strong and difficult to manage that at least five or six 250-plus-pound people are required to restrain the patients. Many times, formal restraint devices are used. The description of the "demon-possessed man" in Luke 8 is therefore a very dramatic, though unfortunately very accurate, description of an individual suffering from acute and serious mental illness. The account of the man possessed by an "evil spirit" in Acts 19:15 is similar in that it describes a man who, because of his condition, was so powerful as to be able to overpower seven sons of Sceva. [This latter account came after the famous verses (vv. 11–12): "God did extraordinary miracles through Paul, so that even handkerchiefs and aprons that had touched him were taken to the sick, and their illnesses were cured and the evil spirits left them." In this case as with others described in this book, though described as "evil spirits," the description is consistent with untreated serious mental illness, although few details are provided].

Even without the severe agitation described in this account, cutting, or much worse, is very common. In Mark 5:5, the man was described as someone who would "cry out and cut himself with stones." Psychotic people do not uncommonly self-injure. I have had many patients essentially perform minor surgeries on themselves because they thought that they were infested with parasites or other foreign entitites. These behaviors are typical of serious mental illness.

The middle part of the story is very interesting for a number of reasons, including that Jesus began to have a discussion with the man's "demons," named "Legion" (v. 30), and only healed the man after transferring the illness to a large herd of pigs, which rushed into the lake. Several questions that people often have about this exchange are: 1) Why did Jesus have a discussion with Legion and transfer Legion to the pigs? Why did he not just cure the man and leave it at that? 2) Does this discussion, and the aftermath in which Legion was transferred to the pigs, not provide evidence that Legion was actually a demon or the devil rather than a mental illness? Regarding the second question, before setting out to write this book I never considered that this story was anything other than the curing of a demon-possessed man. However, what if we were to try to understand this story from the perspective of mental illness? That this man was speaking as Legion is actually wholly consistent with mental illness. Many individuals with severe psychosis develop delusions of having a false identity—for example, that they are kings, presidents, famous actors, rock stars, other political or military leaders, Satan, God, aliens, or the undead. The proper way of interacting with people with these delusions is almost exactly as described in this passage. In fact, Jesus responded to Legion as any psychiatrist would interact with a delusional person. Namely, to understand who they think they are and their purpose, and to try to empathize with and understand them, not challenging their delusion, and not reinforcing it. For example, even first-year psychiatry residents know that the wrong thing to do would be to dismiss a patient's delusion and tell this person that he is not Legion but actually a person, say "Mr. G," with a delusion. Similarly, it would be inappropriate to reinforce their delusion, for example by telling Legion that he has additional information about his identification, such as by appearance or report, in order to gain his trust. In addition, this would serve to help one understand the psychotic person's delusions. As one of my supervisors would often tell me when I was in residency, it is not that delusional people are illogical. Rather, their thinking is very logical once you understand the premises for their beliefs. For example, I had one patient who would wear a winter hat that covered his ears wherever he went. It did not matter the time of year nor whether he was inside or outside, he always wore this hat. It was odd and seemingly illogical, especially in summer when it would have been very uncomfortable to wear a winter cap. Therefore, nobody understood why he was doing this. Everyone just attributed this behavior to his psychotic illness. When I began seeing this patient I noticed the same behavior and figured that there must have been a reason for it. It was during our second session when I learned that this patient thought that all human beings were actually impostors, with their bodies being taken over by an alien race from Jupiter. According to the patient, the way that this alien race took control of peoples' bodies was by sending electronic signals through their ears into their brains. The patient had to cover his ears at all times in order to prevent being taken over by this alien race. Therefore, although at first view this patient's behavior was seemingly illogical, I eventually understood the reason for why he was wearing a cap even in the summer and indoors. It was completely logical, based on what this patient believed. I used this understanding in the treatment and was better able to understand and ally with the patient with this new understanding. Therefore, Jesus simply and appropriately communicated with, and obtained information from, the man.

The second question is, why did Jesus have a discussion with Legion/the man at all? Why did he not just immediately cure him or remove Legion or the mental illness from the man? This is a very important question and point of discussion and, in fact, I believe that the answer is the same regardless of whether this miracle is understood as the healing of a person possessed by a demon or afflicted with untreated serious mental illness. Similar questions are asked about why Jesus, in Mark 8, spit into a blind man's eyes, which only led to the person having partial vision ("I see people; they look like trees walking around" [v. 24]), before putting his hands on the blind man's eyes and fully restoring his sight; or why Jesus, earlier in Luke 8, allowed a severe storm to develop, apparently threatening his and the disciples' lives, before he calmed it.

Of course, Jesus did not have to do anything except to will healing for it to happen, and of course he did not have to even allow the storm to develop. For that matter, Jesus did not have to allow himself to be crucified to be God. However, Jesus *chose* to allow each of these things to happen to demonstrate his omnipotence—that he is God and the Creator, with dominion over all of Creation, including humans, animals, the weather, and even life and death. Jesus's miracles were performed with the explicit purpose of showing unbelieving and doubting humans that he is in fact the Son of God. Therefore, the experiences of watching the healing of the "demon-possessed" man via the transfer of the illness to the pigs, the restoration of sight to the blind man in a multi-step process, and the crucifixion and resurrection of Jesus, were all enhanced by the specific details and process of each miracle. Therefore, how this miracle occurred would be wholly consistent with the understanding that this person was experiencing mental illness, or that he was demon-possessed.

One may still wonder whether this story is about demon possession, rather than about the healing of a mentally ill person. A quick review of the literature, or a quick online search, reveals that nearly all commentaries about these Bible passages, as well as the Bible sub-headings for these passages themselves, almost universally refer to these passages as telling a story about Jesus' healing of a demon-possessed man. In fact, Matthew, Mark and Luke all describe the man as being possessed by a demon. In Mark 5:8, it is recorded that Jesus said "Come out of this man, you impure spirit!" Understanding this point requires an understanding of the context in which the Bible was written. As described before, the inception of medicine, common education, and science was still centuries to millennia away, and unusual phenomena such as mental illness and physical illness were often described in religious or spiritual terms. However, many believe that the Bible is a divinely-inspired document and the Truth—i.e., that it is infallible. Even if the apostles, who were only men, mistakenly referred to people with mental or physical illness as being possessed by demons, Jesus Christ himself used this language. Is it possible that Jesus did not understand mental or physical illness the way that we do now?

Of course not. Jesus, God, and divine inspiration are all-knowing. Therefore, there must be a way to understand why such language was used if this story is not actually about demon possession or exorcisms as we would understand them today. The answers lie in the Bible, and this thesis is strongly supported by this and other passages in the Bible in which words such as "demon" and "spirit" are very loosely used to describe medical or many other phenomena. For example, even Jesus Christ himself was accused of being "demon-possessed" (John 7:20) just because of his wisdom and ability to perform miracles and preach the truth.

Throughout the Bible, there is a clear distinction between how potential medical and psychiatric conditions are discussed compared to how evil works, Satan, magic, sin, or the devil are discussed. For example, in these sections of the Bible (i.e., Luke 8; Mark 5; Matt 8), as well as in Acts 19 (as described above), Luke 7:21 ("At that very time Jesus cured many who had diseases, sicknesses and evil spirits, and gave sight to many who were blind"), Acts 5:16 ("Crowds gathered also from the towns around Jerusalem, bringing their sick and those tormented by impure spirits, and all of them were healed"), Matthew 4:24 ("News about him spread all over Syria, and people brought to him all who were ill with various diseases, those suffering severe pain, the demon-possessed, those having seizures, and the paralyzed; and he healed them"), Matthew 10:8 ("Heal the sick, raise the dead, cleanse those who have leprosy, drive out demons. Freely you have received; freely give"), Luke 13:31–32 ("At that time some Pharisees came to Jesus and said to him, "Leave this place and go somewhere else. Herod wants to kill you." He replied, "Go tell that fox, 'I will keep on driving out demons and healing people today and tomorrow, and on the third day I will reach my goal'"), Mark 3:10–1 ("For he had healed many, so that those with diseases were pushing forward to touch him. Whenever the impure spirits saw him, they fell down before him and cried out, 'You are the Son of God'") and Acts 8:7 ("For with shrieks, impure spirits came out of many, and many who were paralyzed or lame were healed"), the authors described "spirits" in the context of speaking about the healing of physical conditions. This suggests that the "spirits" to which the authors were referring were very possibly related to medical, and in these cases mental, illnesses.

This thesis is also supported by the many specific instances in the New Testament in which very clearly described physical illnesses are themselves described in the context of "spirits" and "demons." For example, in Mark 9, Matthew 17, and Luke 9, Jesus is confronted by the father of a child who suffered from all of the classic signs of a generalized seizure (e.g., foaming at the mouth, becoming unconscious, rigidity, and shaking). Matthew and Luke describe the boy as having a demon, and even Jesus referred to the condition as related to having a "spirit" (Mark 9:25), even though the father clearly said that the boy has "seizures" (Matt 17:15). However, as Jesus is all knowing, he also understood the true nature of this man's condition and chose to explain the situation in a more neutral and culturally appropriate manner, consistent with an ancient, pre-Enlightenment narrative. Obviously, Jesus could not have told the crowd or the man that he would heal his epilepsy. No one would have had any understanding of what that meant, as an understanding of the biological etiology of epilepsy was not understood until recently, even though people understood the phenomenology of seizures.

In Matthew 12, Luke 11, and Mark 3 Jesus was again described as having cured a man who was blind and mute, but who was also still described as being demon-possessed. This passage further underscores how people of this time, before a modern understanding of medicine, science, and biology existed, understood physical phenomena by ascribing abnormalities, including obviously medical illness, to supernatural etiologies. This person, who was supposedly demon-possessed, was not reported in any Gospel to have any behavioral abnormality—he had a purely "physical" condition—yet was still considered to be demon-possessed. Jesus healed him, prompting the Pharisees to accuse him of being an agent of Beelzebub, or Satan. While this accusation was ridiculous for many reasons, Jesus used logical reasoning based on the Pharisee's hypothesis to refute this accusation. Importantly, Jesus did not admit to casting out a true demon (or Satan, the source of all demons). Rather, in an attempt to demonstrate how false the Pharisees' statement really was, he used their own hypothetical situation as an analogy to refute their own argument. To underscore this point, after using the hypothetical act of casting out demons to support his argument, Jesus used other analogies, such as thieves entering the house of a very strong person.

Similar discussions can be applied to the many other instances in which people were healed of "spirits" or "demons" though much less information was given. These include the "demon-possessed" (Matt 9:32) man who was just described as mute; the "exorcisms" performed at sunset after Jesus healed Peter's mother-in-law as described in Mark 1, Luke 4, and Matthew 8; Mary Magdalene, who was reportedly cured of "seven demons" (Luke 8:2; Mark 16:9); the events of Mark 6:7, "Calling the Twelve to him, he began to send them out two by two and gave them authority over impure spirits" and Luke 10:17, "The seventy-two returned with joy and said, "Lord, even the demons submit to us in your name"; the female slave who was healed by Paul in Acts 16; and the daughter of the Canaanite woman who asked Jesus to heal her daughter (Matt 15; Mark 7). Of note, in the latter miracle, Jesus was reported as saying, in Mark 7:29, that "the demon has left your daughter" after he healed the daughter. In this case, it is again understood that Jesus could not describe the women's daughter as having a mental or physical illness as no one would have understood that. Rather, he described her healing in a way that the mother would understand. This is actually a standard means of communicating about medical conditions. For example, even in modern times, different cultures have ways of understanding and describing mental illness. These may range from the general such as "nervios," which may apply to a wide range of conditions among Latino individuals, to the more specific such as taijin kyofusho ("interpersonal fear disorder" in Japanese), which applies to the avoidance of social or interpersonal situations due to concerns about inadequancy.[1] Therefore, the authors of the Bible, and Jesus, would very frequently describe both physical and mental illnesses with language such as "spirits" and "demon possession" even when they were very possibly describing mental and physical conditions or diseases.

Nowadays, nearly everyone understands that congenital physical disabilities, for example blindness or paralysis, are biological and/or genetic in nature, and have nothing to do with

1. American Psychiatric Association, *Diagnostic and Statistical Manual*, 833–37.

morality, sinfulness, or faith. However, in Biblical times people still very much associated medical conditions with morality, sinfulness, faith, or the supernatural in general, including the disciples. Jesus himself taught his disciples not to confuse medical illness with anything supernatural. For example, in John 9, Jesus and his disciples came across a blind man. Jesus's own disciples, still very much learning and understanding the true meaning of Jesus, God, sin, redemption, and human nature, asked Jesus, "Rabbi, who sinned, this man or his parents, that he was born blind?" (v. 2). Jesus clearly answered that this person's disability had nothing to do with sin or anything besides physical illness: "'Neither this man nor his parents sinned,' said Jesus, 'but this happened so that the works of God might be displayed in him'" (v. 3). It is my assertion that mental illness in the Bible is no different. The difference is that, in modern times, many people still believe that mental illness is related to sin or morality, rather than biology and genetics, like physical illness is.

Why would modern society have such a primitive understanding of mental illness? This is in part because science has not revealed as much about the causes of mental illness as it has about physical illness. However, I would also submit that much of the responsibility lies with society and its unwillingness to integrate the Bible into mainstream society. The Bible is many things, including a guide to morality, a historical text, and the foundation of Judeo-Christianity, but also has many important scientific revelations. Much of what we now readily accept and know about the physical world was quite clearly described in the Bible, often centuries to millennia before being widely accepted or otherwise proven. For example, Earth is clearly described as a spherical object in Isaiah 40:22, and as free-floating in space in Job 26:7, many millennia before the roundness of Earth and its gravitational orbit were widely understood. The general time course of events of the creation of the universe and life on Earth are summarized in Genesis 1, many millennia before much of what we now understand about the beginning of life and the universe was understood. Finally, the cycle of evaporation of water from the ocean to falling on land—not understood until very recently—is described in Amos 9:6.

As the Bible explains physical phenomena and allows us to understand how people from Jesus's time misunderstood physical and mental illness, so too can we depend on what the Bible says about Satan, evil, and true "demons" by examining instances in which demons or Satan, the source of all demons and evil, were actually involved. Nowhere is this more clear than during the temptation of Jesus, as told in Mark 1, Luke 4, and Matthew 4, when Jesus, confronted by Satan, specifically referred to him as such. For example, in Matthew 4:10, Jesus says "Away with you, Satan! For it is written: 'Worship the Lord your God, and serve him only.'" In this story, in which Jesus was directly confronted by Satan himself, it is clear that Satan's single and only power is over evil, which can only manifest as temptation. Why would Jesus not refer to the man in Luke 8, Mark 5, and Matthew 8 as being possessed by the devil or Satan if he was in fact possessed?

Satan was given no authority over nature and cannot afflict people with diseases in any direct manner. Nowhere in the Bible was Satan able to infiltrate or control a person, except indirectly, when, by their own free will, one would accept Satan and temptation into their life. There is no precedent in the Bible for demon possession, except as a way for people in historical, pre-Enlightenment times to understand or describe behavior for which they had no other explanation. Even in the story of Job, Satan required special permission to destroy Job's life and everything around him. Additionally, God strictly forbade Satan from any direct influence on Job: "Very well, then, everything he has is in your power, but on the man himself do not lay a finger" (Job 1:12). God eventually allowed one exception to this rule, by allowing Satan to afflict Job's body only, as in Job 2:6: "The Lord said to Satan, 'Very well, then, he is in your hands; but you must spare his life.'" However, even in this case, it is very clear that God would not allow Satan the ability to infiltrate or control a person's mind, except indirectly, when, by their own free will, one would accept Satan and temptation into their life. Even during the fall, Satan could only tempt Eve. He had no other power. Only through Eve and Adam's free will was Satan able to influence them. This is the promise of the Bible, Creation, the fall, Job, and Jesus Christ. God gave humankind free will. And God does not have favorites. He loves every human being equally and has demonstrated through the stories of Adam and Eve and Job that while temptation and nature, including severe physical illness, may bring tragedy and desolation, God has never and will never allow Satan to have dominion over our minds or free will. In other words, Satan, who by definition is the source of all demons and evil spirits, cannot infiltrate a person's mind.

> But when the Pharisees heard this, they said, "It is only by Beelzebul, the prince of demons, that this fellow drives out demons." Jesus knew their thoughts and said to them, "Every kingdom divided against itself will be ruined, and every city or household divided against itself will not stand. If Satan drives out Satan, he is divided against himself. How then can his kingdom stand? And if I drive out demons by Beelzebul, by whom do your people drive them out? So then, they will be your judges. But if it is by the Spirit of God that I drive out demons, then the kingdom of God has come upon you." (Matt 12:24–8)

There are numerous other examples in the Bible in which Satan, sin, evil works, or "real" demons were actually involved, and in these cases, the Bible makes it clear what these passages were about. For example, in John 6:70–71, after many disciples left Jesus because they were not happy with the Truth of the Spirit that Jesus was preaching, and Peter was bragging about the twelve apostles, Jesus corrected him by saying, "'Have I not chosen you, the Twelve? Yet one of you is a devil!' (He meant Judas, the son of Simon Iscariot, who, though one of the Twelve, was later to betray him.)" In this case, Jesus was clearly describing the sin of Judas's deception and betrayal, which was fully motivated by Satan. In addition, in Acts 5:3–4 when describing the deceit and greed by how Ananias was dealing with his offerings to the believers, Peter said

> Ananias, how is it that Satan has so filled your heart that
> you have lied to the Holy Spirit and have kept for yourself
> some of the money you received for the land? Didn't it
> belong to you before it was sold? And after it was sold,
> wasn't the money at your disposal? What made you think
> of doing such a thing? You have not lied just to human
> beings but to God.

Again, Peter is clearly describing the spirit of sin and evil. Finally, in Ecclesiastes, Solomon describes "madness" in the context of sin and evil: "Then I applied myself to the understanding of wisdom, and also of madness and folly, but I learned that this, too, is a chasing after the wind" (1:17), and "This is the evil in everything that happens under the sun: The same destiny overtakes all. The hearts of people, moreover, are full of evil and there is madness in their hearts while they live, and afterward they join the dead" (9:3). I will discuss the powers of Satan in much greater detail in chapter 11.

Therefore, in the story of the "demon-possessed" man of Luke 8, Mark 5, and Matthew 8, it is possible that Jesus was clearly and quite explicitly not referring to the devil or Satan or any "evil" spirit, or else he would have said so. It is very possible that Jesus, who is all knowing, understood the true nature of this man's condition and chose to explain the situation in a more neutral and culturally appropriate manner, consistent with an ancient, pre-Enlightenment understanding. Obviously, Jesus could not have told the crowd or the man that he would heal this man's schizophrenia. No one would have had any understanding of what that meant, as the term "schizophrenia" was not coined until the twentieth century.[2]

The latter part of the story describes how the pig farmers told other townspeople about what had happened. The people then went to see the man, who had been healed and was acting normally, for themselves. Interestingly, they asked Jesus to leave due to being "overcome with fear" (v. 37). While shock and awe were common reactions to Jesus's miracles, the fear that the people

2. Heckers, *Bleuler and the Neurobiology of Schizophrenia*, 1131.

of Gerasenes had, and that they asked him to leave their town, was unusual. One main difference between this miracle and the others that Jesus performed was that Jesus demonstrated that he had dominion over the herd of pigs, as opposed to only humans. While this should only have reinforced the miracle and further confirmed the omnipotence and dominion of Jesus, the Gerasenes were unable to see the miracle for what it was. Rather than accept and glorify Jesus as a doer of miracles, omnipotent, and the Savior of Mankind, they were completely blind to the miracle and, like many other people, unwilling to accept Jesus.

CHAPTER 9

The Miracle of the "Exorcism"
at the Synagogue in Capernaum
(Mark 1, Luke 4)

———————

The story of Mark 1 and Luke 4 is similar to the story of Luke 8, Mark 5, and Matthew 8 and is often referred to as an exorcism. For this book, I will refer to the Mark 1 passage, though the accounts in Mark 1 and Luke 4 are very similar. As with the miracle of the (Gadarene) demoniac, examining this story from the perspective of serious mental illness could provide a great deal of understanding about serious mental illness. As stated above, it is important to iterate that my goal in this chapter is not to change the reader's view that the Miracle of the Exorcism at the Synagogue in Capernaum is about serious mental illness per se, but rather to use this great miracle to enhance what we understand about serious mental illness. I will undertake to do so now.

This miracle occurred relatively early in Jesus's ministry. Jesus was teaching on the Sabbath in a synagogue. A man who was "possessed by an impure spirit" (v. 23) yelled "What do you want with us, Jesus of Nazareth? Have you come to destroy us? I know who you are—the Holy One of God!" (v. 24). Jesus very sternly told the man to be quiet and ordered the illness to leave the man. The man then shook "violently" (v. 26), yelled, and was healed.

Luke referred to the man as having a "demon" (v. 35) and Mark as an "impure spirit" (v. 26). However, this description is also completely consistent with mental illness, and in particular with an individual with an untreated, severe psychotic disorder such as schizophrenia or a severe form of bipolar disorder. The man in this Bible passage acted very similarly to how people with severe auditory hallucinations may act. When auditory hallucinations are severe, they can completely take over a person's sensorium. To an outsider, these people will appear to be preoccupied, engaging in very active, sometimes incoherent conversations with the sounds or voices that they hear. They may have minimal awareness of other people in their environment. Their functioning may be severely impeded by frequent emotional and behavioral responses to their hallucinations, and at times they may respond to commands given by the hallucinations. Their movements and speech often appear unmodulated. Their motor behaviors may be atypically accelerated, bizarre, and ritualistic, sometimes to the point of complete exhaustion.

The behavior of the man in this passage is consistent with all of these behaviors. He starts by yelling at Jesus in an unmodulated manner that would be inappropriate for a quiet teaching session in the synagogue. The man was paranoid and accused Jesus of wanting to destroy him. Jesus, knowing full well what manner of illness afflicted this man, sternly told the man to be quiet, which would be the appropriate first step for a psychiatrist in dealing with any severely agitated, paranoid patient, and then healed him. After a very brief final period of unmodulated screaming and motor behavior, the man was cured.

Many of the discussion points about the man in Luke 8, Mark 5, and Matthew 8 described in chapter 8 apply to this passage as well—for example, that the person's symptoms and behavior were very consistent with those that would be observed in someone with untreated, serious mental illness, and that Jesus told the illness to leave the man in order to demonstrate his dominion to the people who were present, rather than just willing it to happen.

Further, this story is often referred to as an exorcism. Therefore, as we near the conclusion of this book, I will build on all of the previous discussions about how accounts of "spirits" and "demon possession" in the Bible reveal a great deal about serious mental illness, and directly address how we could understand them using a post-Enlightenment, modern narrative. There are two key questions that underscore the theme of this whole book and require answers in order for the thesis of this book to be supported: 1) Are exorcisms real, at least in modern times? 2) Does whether we describe these events as exorcisms of demons or treatment of mental illness make any difference as to how miraculous were Jesus's actions? The second question is easier to answer than the first. As described in the introduction, the categories of mental illness described in this book are modern categories that reflect post-Enlightenment rationality. The Bible comes from a different narrative culture that could not explain things in terms of Enlightenment rationality. For example, many of the stories in chapters 8 and 9 about exorcisms and demon possession reflect the narrative of the ancient world. From the perspective of modern rationality, we understand these individuals' behavior in a different way— perhaps as serious mental illness. When reading this book and understanding the Bible stories, one must recognize that these two narratives (pre- and post-Enlightenment) produce two narrative assumptions that are different but readily and largely overlap. If we keep clear about the two different rationalities we can honor them both. This, however, requires of us an honest recognition that the two narrative perspectives are not incommensurate, and we, as believers, are in some way participants in both worlds. It is imperative on us, if we are going to make any progress towards dealing with serious mental illness and stigma, to work at seeing how these two narratives relate and illuminate each other rather than to adjudicate on the truth of these stories.

In other words, whether we understand these miracles as exorcisms or treatment of mental illness seems to make no difference as to the importance or impact of the miracles themselves. As demonstrated, all of the behaviors ascribed to demon possession seem to be present in primarily untreated, serious mental illness, and even worse. Mental illness is biological, heritable, severe, and usually chronic. Jesus's dominion over all of heaven and earth and his ability to perform miracles seem to be demonstrated whether he exorcised demons or cured individuals with mental or physical illnesses. Therefore, in the opinion of the author, of course Jesus Christ exorcised demons and Satan, in the greatest way possible. He allowed himself to be crucified and then resurrected. All other miracles, phenomena, and stories are meant to confirm and lead us to this revelation. The true miracle, or "exorcism" if you will, performed by Jesus is his resurrection and subsequent victory over death, not his casting out of spirits or healing people who are blind or have other physical or mental conditions.

This point is perhaps best illustrated by what Jesus said himself during one of his subsequent miracles, as told in Mark 2, Luke 5, and Matthew 9. In this very well-known story, Jesus was preaching in a house. The house was very full. Several men had a friend who was paralyzed and whom they wanted to set before Jesus. Since they were unable to enter the house through the doorway, they lowered him through the roof. Jesus, seeing their persistence and faith, forgave the paralyzed man's sins. The Pharisees and other teachers began to think very critically of Jesus, upset that he was, in their opinion, blaspheming God by forgiving sins. Jesus sensed their thoughts and asked them whether they thought that it would be easier to forgive someone's sins or cure their paralysis. In order to demonstrate that Jesus has dominion over all things heavenly and earthly, Jesus then healed the paralytic man, to the amazement of everyone in attendance.

Another example is at the resurrection of Lazarus of Bethany described in John 11. Initially, Jesus and his disciples were sent word by Lazarus's sisters Mary and Martha that Lazarus was ill. Jesus waited two days then decided to go to Judea to "awaken" Lazarus. The disciples told Jesus that it would be good for Lazarus to sleep in order to recover from his illness. They also did not want

Jesus to go to Judea out of concern for his safety. They very clearly still did not understand who Jesus really is and why he had to go to Judea. Therefore, Jesus said,

> "Our friend Lazarus has fallen asleep; but I am going there to wake him up." His disciples replied, "Lord, if he sleeps, he will get better." Jesus had been speaking of his death, but his disciples thought he meant natural sleep. So then he told them plainly, "Lazarus is dead, and for your sake I am glad I was not there, so that you may believe. But let us go to him." (vv. 11–15).

Jesus knew that he had to raise Lazarus from the dead to enhance the faith of his disciples whom he would soon leave on Earth and depend upon to continue his ministry of humankind.

When Jesus arrived, he saw how sad everyone was, including the townspeople, Martha, and Mary. To Martha he said,

> "Your brother will rise again." Martha answered, "I know he will rise again in the resurrection at the last day." Jesus said to her, "I am the resurrection and the life. The one who believes in me will live, even though they die; and whoever lives by believing in me will never die. Do you believe this?" "Yes, Lord," she replied, "I believe that you are the Messiah, the Son of God, who is to come into the world." (vv. 23–27).

Shortly thereafter, Mary said to Jesus, "Lord, if you had been here, my brother would not have died" (v. 32). As the disciples still did not understand who Jesus is, Martha and Mary did not understand the power of Jesus Christ. After being asked to see where Lazarus' body had been placed, "Jesus wept" (v. 35).

These two words are some of the most powerful words in the Bible and some of the most meaningful. After seeing Jesus in tears, the people who were present remarked, "See how he loved him!" (v. 36), implying that Jesus was tearful because he was sad that Lazarus had died. However, the real meaning of Jesus's tears is made apparent by the next four verses:

> But some of them said, "Could not he who opened the
> eyes of the blind man have kept this man from dying?"
> Jesus, once more deeply moved, came to the tomb. It was
> a cave with a stone laid across the entrance. "Take away
> the stone," he said. "But, Lord," said Martha, the sister of
> the dead man, "by this time there is a bad odor, for he
> has been there four days." Then Jesus said, "Did I not tell
> you that if you believe, you will see the glory of God?"
> (vv. 37–40)

Jesus was not tearful because he missed Lazarus. What these verses clarify is that Jesus was tearful because the disciples, Martha, Mary, and the townspeople, despite all of Jesus' miracles and everything he had done, still had no understanding of who Jesus is. They were focused on a physical understanding of the situation and of Jesus, rather than on a spiritual understanding.

The relevance of this story to the current discussion is that many times we, believers, fall victim to believing physical phenomena more than the true, supernatural teachings and attributes of Jesus and his message. In this story, Jesus is clearly trying to teach everyone present and who reads the story for all time that healing a paralytic person, or any other physical miracle, is not in and of itself the message of Jesus Christ but meant to enhance the true message, miracle, and story of Jesus Christ—namely, that Jesus Christ was crucified and rose from the dead on the third day to abolish our sins, thereby giving eternal life to all who believe in him. Of course Jesus Christ exorcised demons and Satan, in the greatest way possible. He allowed himself to be crucified and then resurrected. All other miracles, phenomena, and stories are meant to confirm and lead us to this revelation. The true miracle, or "exorcism" if you will, performed by Jesus is his resurrection and subsequent victory over death, not his casting out of spirits or healing people who are blind or have other physical or mental conditions.

We now come to the first question: Are exorcisms real, at least in modern times? To this point I have provided evidence to suggest that many cases in the Bible in which spirits or demons were invoked to describe unusual behaviors or illnesses could also be accounted for by mental or physical illness. However, exorcisms, demon possession or even simply miraculous religious or spiritual healings of physical conditions (often paralysis) occur regularly in both developed and less developed countries. Even if we believe that all of these stories from the Bible in which spirits or demons were invoked to describe unusual behaviors or illnesses involved people with bona fide mental or physical illnesses, how do we explain the countless "miraculous" healings that have occurred in modern times? Are we to believe that there are hundreds or more people on Earth who have the gift of healing, the same way that Jesus Christ did? Or is it possible that demon possession exists in modern times? Is there another explanation?

Many of these so-called exorcisms or miraculous religious or spiritual healings are similar. Usually, an extremely agitated, supposedly paralyzed, or otherwise hysterical person is brought before a religious or spiritual leader, who breathes on, touches, and/ or prays on the afflicted person. In the case of paralysis, people often stand up from wheelchairs in a dramatic fashion. In the case of an exorcism or healing of other spiritual or mental condition, the person's affect immediately changes from one of intensity, being upset, and hysterics to one of calm and a newfound sense of thinking clearly. Sometimes people with virtually no affect, or who are completely mute and unresponsive, become hysterically happy and tearful with appreciation. All cases are high drama. As a psychiatrist, I do not believe that these events are exorcisms or spiritual/miraculous healings of any sort. Many of them are likely staged and acted in an attempt to dishonestly receive money (i.e., in psychiatric parlance these would be described as "malingering" in that they have a clear secondary gain—namely, the tangible gain of money).

Those that are not explicitly acted or dishonest are, in my estimation, related to a group of disorders referred to as factitious or somatic symptom (previously somatoform) disorders, and the religious individuals involved are simply unaware or accepting of this fact, many of them sincerely believing that they are exorcising demons or simply trying to help individuals with factitious disorders.[1] Factitious disorders are psychiatric disorders characterized by medical or psychiatric symptoms that are consciously produced but have an unconscious motivation (such as consciously faking a paralysis for a reason such as primary gain, i.e., the psychological need to play the sick role and receive attention and caring). Somatic symptom disorders are similar to factitious disorders in that the motivation tends to be unconscious. Somatic symptom disorders are different from factitious disorders in that the medical or behavioral symptoms are unconsciously produced. Somatic symptom disorders include what was previously referred to as hypochondriasis (an unwarranted fear of having a medical condition out of proportion to the medical findings) as well as conversion disorders (as described below). Henceforth, I will only refer to somatic symptom disorders, though the discussion and arguments would be similar for individuals with factitious disorders.

Individuals with somatic symptom disorders often have "ego deficits," to use psychodynamic parlance, which refers to deficits in emotional and behavioral traits such as mood stability, anxiety tolerance, reality testing, self-awareness, and impulse control. Having such deficits leads to an inability to interact with the world in a standard, more adaptive way, and leads to primitive behavior. This behavior can take the form of believing one has a disease when one does not, otherwise known as hypochondriasis. These people are convinced that they have a medical condition that is incommensurate with the evidence for one. This behavior can also take the form of symptoms of a medical condition (aka "conversion" symptoms) that are incompatible with the clinical evidence.[2] This type of condition is exemplified by pseudo- or psychogenic seizures. Pseudoseizures are seizure-like activity (i.e., usually a person shaking their whole body in a seizure-like manner) that are not caused by a seizure disorder. These symptoms are produced by

1. American Psychiatric Association, *Diagnostic and Statistical Manual*, 309–27.

2. American Psychiatric Association, *Diagnostic and Statistical Manual*, 309–27.

the person to seem as if they are having a seizure. That is, there is no direct biological cause or reason for these people to have these movements. People who have pseudoseizures are very susceptible to suggestion and often completely believe they are having bona-fide epileptic seizures, even though they are not. Most laypeople have some sense of what a real seizure looks like, and so individuals can make pseudoseizures appear very similar to real seizures. Further, while most pseudoseizures are readily identifiable by an experienced physician as being unrelated to a seizure disorder due to several telltale signs of pseudoseizures (e.g., remaining conscious during a full tonic-clonic or "grand mal" seizure), they can be quite deceiving, especially to someone who is not a physician. In addition, even though they are not epileptic seizures, they can still be very distressing and dramatic.

The motivation for pseudoseizures can be primary (i.e., psychological, aka "the sick role") or secondary (e.g., wanting to receive a drug of abuse, such as diazepam, or wanting to be able to claim to have a medical problem severe enough to warrant receiving disability payments). Consequently, while pseudoseizures are usually not responsive to standard prophylactic medications, they are often very responsive to medications that are given immediately to abort a seizure, such as diazepam or lorazepam. The reason why pseudoseizures would respond so robustly to immediate interventions can be because the patients think this will convince medical personnel that they are really having seizures, or, such as in the case of someone who just wants a drug of abuse, because they have received what they want. Either way, such conditions are very debilitating and severe and are in fact classified as psychiatric conditions, though of a different nature than conditions such as psychosis, schizophrenia, depression, anxiety, and bipolar disorder. Individuals with symptoms of somatic symptom disorders, such as pseudoseizures, are often admitted to medical hospitals and receive extensive workups that can lead to iatrogenic complications (i.e., medical problems that are a result of the testing or treatment of a condition, such as developing an infection from having an intravenous catheter) and can cost many thousands of dollars. These people are, depending on the motivation for the seizures, often very resistant to standard, prophylactic treatments such as antiepileptic medications (which is one strong piece of evidence that a seizure is actually a pseudoseizure).

People with pseudoseizures often respond very strongly to immediate treatments of a different type. This is referred to as a "flight into health" and typically occurs after an interaction with a new physician, many times one who is in training and presents a naïve and unrealistically optimistic perspective about these patients' conditions. These providers are inappropriately drawn into the patient's disorder and feel that all the patient needs in order to get over their pseudoseizures is a greater level of caring and attention that, in the mind of an inexperienced physician, more experienced physicians cannot provide because they are cynical, jaded, or just too busy. The patient, who is in need of attention and caring, immediately responds, though inappropriately. The patients quickly develop hypertrophied positive feelings towards the new physician (aka a positive "transference"), and some of the patient's symptoms may go away. Unfortunately, the symptoms often quickly return since the need for attention and caring on the part of the patient is, by definition, disordered and beyond what anyone can provide. These needs are often a response to a lack of attention, caring, and love in one's childhood, and in more serious cases overt neglect and abuse, and so have woven themselves into the fabric of the patient's emotional makeup, and are therefore very resistant to change. That is, no amount of genuine love, caring, and attention can make up for the years of emotional abuse and negligence often experienced by these people. In many cases, after the patient's initial rapid remission, they almost as quickly relapse, leaving the patient, family, and providers feeling defeated and demoralized.

I would submit that modern "demon possession" of the type for which people obtain exorcisms is very analogous and similar. Indeed, most people who see religious healers or exorcists are likely to be familiar with the Bible and other ancient texts and accounts of "demon possession." Many have substantial and important psychiatric conditions, such as depression and anxiety, for which they need treatment. However, these readily treatable conditions may be severely complicated by the additional and severe need for attention and caring, as well as ego deficits, that typify these patients who seek out exorcists. Many of them may also have tried and failed standard psychiatric treatments. They are likely demoralized, downtrodden individuals, possibly spiritually lost, with a strong need for attention and caring. Furthermore, similar to individuals with pseudoseizures, these individuals may demonstrate more severe and bizarre symptoms that resemble psychosis or mania, but which are not. They may report delusions or hallucinations, speaking with spirits and ghosts, or communicating with alien beings when they really are not experiencing these things. They may alternatively be isolated, asocial, and severely oppositional and socially inappropriate. They may simply be mute but for no biological reason. Since psychiatry still has no objective means by which to diagnosis mental disorders—psychiatric diagnoses are still made on the basis of observation and what patients and their families report—feigning symptoms of more serious mental illness, consciously or unconsciously, is not difficult. Psychiatrists are frequently called on to help manage people with these sorts of conditions. Unfortunately, these individuals are often quite resistant to standard therapies that work for the majority of psychiatric patients. Typically, these patients spend several years seeing numerous psychologists and psychiatrists, trying all sorts of different types of medication and psychotherapies, with little to no relief. Many of them will be hospitalized and receive more significant treatments such as electroconvulsive therapy (aka "shock treatment"), with little to no benefit. These patients' treatment resistance and functional impairment take a toll on them, their families, and their medical providers. This leaves everyone involved feeling very frustrated and impatient, forced to search for all types of "miraculous" remedies, including religious remedies, such as exorcisms, with unrealistic expectations, vulnerable to the ingenuine or unknowing people who may populate these realms. For those patients who find their way to exorcists, similar to the situation with people who have feigned physical conditions, these people become caught up in the drama of an exorcism or laying on of hands. These patients' suggestibility, need for attention, and general ego deficits make them respond robustly, inappropriately, and "miraculously" to spiritual healers may themselves be either dishonest or prone to hysterical behavior. People jump to the conclusion that these people must have been demon-possessed or exorcised in order to heal so rapidly. However, in almost all cases, after the patient's initial rapid remission, they generally quickly relapse to their original behaviors, leaving the patient, family, and providers feeling defeated and demoralized.

Therefore, in the opinion of this author, exorcisms and "demon possession" from modern times can be better accounted for by somatic symptom disorders and/or just pure deceit. This is supported by the story of the man from Mark 1 who was "possessed by an impure spirit" (v. 23). His behavior was very consistent with that of a man suffering from untreated serious mental illness, and Jesus Christ cured him in a miraculous way. Importantly, that the man had a serious mental illness, rather than a spirit or demon, in no way changes the message of the story nor the meaning of this miracle, nor does it affect the story of Jesus Christ in any way. Jesus has clearly demonstrated his sovereignty over demons (i.e., Satan, the source of all demons) with the temptation as well as by his resurrection and abolishment of death. Rather, understanding this miracle as the healing of a person with a serious mental illness, such as schizophrenia, provides an informative account of mental illness in Biblical times and allows for a discussion of the invalidity and/or false promises of those in modern times who proclaim to be able to perform exorcisms and spiritual healing. This message, in addition to the message of Jesus Christ's dominion over all of Creation, is a timeless message that fits perfectly into the narrative of the Bible as a template and guide for living an informed, healthy life, free from perverse ideas and focused on the Truth of God and his Creation.

Interestingly, as I described in chapter 1 and in this chapter, many people who have read earlier version of this book have told me that it is somewhat challenging to try to understand chapters 8 and 9 through the lens of serious mental illness because that could suggest that two miracles of Jesus Christ that have always been considered to be exorcisms and demon possession could potentially be the healing of mental illness. Some also suggest that the interpretation of serious mental illness "takes away" from these miracles. However, an equal number of people who have read earlier versions of this book have actually had no problem with describing the exorcisms from chapters 8 and 9 of this book as serious mental illness but have found it much more challenging to understand that people such as Moses, Jeremiah, Elijah, Job, Jonah, and Naomi may have experienced some sort of mental illness or suicidal thoughts. I was initially unable to understand why this would be the case. Then, I put myself in the shoes of someone who has less experience with mental illness and realized that, as described in chapter 1, many Christian believers also believe in a false equivalence between moral weakness / sin and mental illness based on the agitation, dysphoria, and sometimes overt aggression, violence, anger, hostility, and belligerence of some people with serious mental illness especially when untreated. To these individuals, saying that the "demon-possessed" men described in chapters 8 and 9 had serious mental illness is completely plausible since demon possession and serious mental illness can, at times, both be associated with undesirable behaviors. Many people simply equate mental illness with bad, sinful, or otherwise undesirable behavior. To these people, it would be logical to think that demon possession and mental illness are equivalent, since, by definition, Satan is the source of all demons.

However, based on extensive and repeated readings of the accounts of the miracle of the "exorcism" at the Synagogue in Capernaum and the miracle of the (Gadarene) demoniac I am unable to find any description of a sinful act committed by either individual. This evidence argues against any potential equivalence between mental illness and sin/evil (aka "demon possession") and further supports the thesis of this book that some instances of demon possession and exorcisms as described in the Bible could be better explained by occurring in the context of mental illness, and that this could reveal a great deal of information about the Biblical view of mental illness.

CHAPTER 10

The Bible and Sorcery, Spirits, and Witchcraft

———————

While all previous chapters have based their discussions on one particular Bible story, the next two chapters will focus less on a specific Bible passage and more on the sum total of what the Bible says about the topics of sorcery, spirits, witchcraft, Satan, and other supernatural phenomena not directly related to God, Jesus, the Holy Spirit, or the disciples. What the Bible says about these phenomena is unambiguous and supports the thesis of this book in an important way. While not directly speaking to mental illness, as all of the previous chapters did, the passages in the Bible about these phenomena do directly address how we should interpret exorcisms and spiritual healing. Additionally, as the reader will notice, the short quotations from the Bible that speak to sorcery and witchcraft are extremely unambiguous and clear. Therefore, little commentary will be required to explain or contextualize these statements.

Sorcery is addressed multiple times throughout the Old and New Testaments. The first time is in Exodus 22. In this chapter, only two chapters after God revealed his Ten Commandments,

God is dictating to Moses his covenant or agreement with Israel. In as plainly stated a rule as can be, God tells Moses, "Do not allow a sorceress to live" (v. 18). In other words, God is saying that the practice of sorcery is an evil that must be avoided.

Moses repeats this rule in Deuteronomy 18 while delivering a sermon to Israel shortly before his death and before Israel's entry into the promised land,

> Let no one be found among you who sacrifices their son or daughter in the fire, who practices divination or sorcery, interprets omens, engages in witchcraft, or casts spells, or who is a medium or spiritist or who consults the dead. Anyone who does these things is detestable to the Lord; because of these same detestable practices the Lord your God will drive out those nations before you. (vv. 10–12)

Once again, it is made clear to Israel that any sort of practice of or belief in these types of supernatural phenomena, including spirits, witchcraft, sorcery, etc., is strictly forbidden, wrong, and inconsistent with Biblical teachings and Scripture.

Consistent with the theme that engaging in supernatural phenomena, including spirits, witchcraft, or sorcery, is antithetical to God, his message, and divine power is the assertion in 1 Chronicles 10:13–14 that "Saul died because he was unfaithful to the Lord; he did not keep the word of the Lord and even consulted a medium for guidance, and did not inquire of the Lord. So the Lord put him to death and turned the kingdom over to David son of Jesse." Although being specifically chosen by God to lead Israel, King Saul had to die and lose his kingship over Israel. The author of 1 Chronicles clearly indicated why this was the case—namely, because he was unfaithful to God, consulted a medium for guidance, and did not consult God. What an amazing statement that of everything that King Saul did that was evil, sinful, or against God, the one thing that the author of 1 Chronicles chose to include in this passage was that King Saul chose to consult a medium. The writer of 1 Chronicles was aware of the evil and perversity that originate from spirits, witchcraft, or sorcery, and found it important to emphasize these facts.

The New Testament continues these themes. In Acts 8, Peter and John were confronted by a sorcerer named Simon who lived in Samaria. Peter was quick to condemn him: "You have no part or share in this ministry, because your heart is not right before God. Repent of this wickedness and pray to the Lord in the hope that he may forgive you for having such a thought in your heart. For I see that you are full of bitterness and captive to sin" (vv. 21–23). In this exchange, Peter makes clear that believing in or ascribing to any spirit besides the Holy Spirit and God is contrary to the teachings of Jesus Christ.

In Acts 13, Paul and Barnabas were in Cyprus and were challenged by Elymas the sorcerer (also referred to as Bar-Jesus). Paul made it clear what he thinks about sorcery, witchcraft, and evil spirits: "You are a child of the devil and an enemy of everything that is right! You are full of all kinds of deceit and trickery. Will you never stop perverting the right ways of the Lord? Now the hand of the Lord is against you. You are going to be blind for a time, not even able to see the light of the sun" (vv. 10–11). Paul's teaching here is clear. Anyone who claims any supernatural power or spiritual understanding that is not directly related to Jesus Christ is not a follower of Jesus Christ's teaching.

Paul continued to condemn people who worship or spiritually participate in anything besides worship of Jesus Christ in his epistles to the Corinthians—

> Consider the people of Israel: Do not those who eat the sacrifices participate in the altar? Do I mean then that food sacrificed to an idol is anything, or that an idol is anything? No, but the sacrifices of pagans are offered to demons, not to God, and I do not want you to be participants with demons. You cannot drink the cup of the Lord and the cup of demons too; you cannot have a part in both the Lord's table and the table of demons. Are we trying to arouse the Lord's jealousy? Are we stronger than he? (1 Cor 10:18–22)

—and to Timothy—

> The Spirit clearly says that in later times some will aban-
> don the faith and follow deceiving spirits and things
> taught by demons. Such teachings come through hypo-
> critical liars, whose consciences have been seared as with
> a hot iron. (1 Tim 4:1–2)

In Galatians 5, Paul goes on to group witchcraft with idolatry,
sexual immorality, and many other of the most severe, perverse,
sinful acts:

> The acts of the flesh are obvious: sexual immorality, im-
> purity and debauchery; idolatry and witchcraft; hatred,
> discord, jealousy, fits of rage, selfish ambition, dissen-
> sions, factions and envy; drunkenness, orgies, and the
> like. I warn you, as I did before, that those who live like
> this will not inherit the kingdom of God. (vv. 19–21)

Finally, in Revelation 21 and 22, the final and concluding
chapters of the whole Bible, John provides a final reinforcement of
the danger and evils of sorcery, witchcraft, and false spirits. After a
full book of apocalyptic imagery and destruction, John concludes
with chapters 21 and 22 and a promise both of Jesus's second coming and of the condemnation of evildoers: "But the cowardly, the
unbelieving, the vile, the murderers, the sexually immoral, those
who practice magic arts, the idolaters and all liars—they will be
consigned to the fiery lake of burning sulfur. This is the second
death" (Rev 21:8); "Outside are the dogs, those who practice magic
arts, the sexually immoral, the murderers, the idolaters and everyone who loves and practices falsehood" (Rev 22:15). As did Paul
before him, John dramatically groups the practice of "magic arts"
along with the most severe, reprobate sins, including murder, sexual immorality, and idolatry. In no uncertain terms, John contrasts
good with evil and makes clear that spirituality that is not clearly
Christ-centered is contrary to Christianity and Jesus's teachings.

The Bible, in no uncertain way, repeatedly condemns any sort
of witchcraft, magic, or related spiritual behavior. The exorcising
of demons and anything related to supernatural phenomena are

antithetical to what is taught in the Bible, are against God, and are listed among the worst sins.

CHAPTER 11

Temptation Is the Limit of Satan's Power, and How We Know This

---

A s described in chapter 10, previous chapters of this book have been written with a focus on passages and stories from the Bible that more directly describe or address serious mental illness. This chapter will also focus on a fuller discussion of a topic that was brought up in previous chapters and supports the thesis of this book by providing a slightly more theological perspective on mental illness.

In this chapter I will expound on a discussion begun in chapter 8 about the extent of Satan's powers. In particular, by examining Biblical accounts of Satan, I will provide further evidence that Satan has no power over creation. Satan is very powerful, and evil is real, for sure. However, I will demonstrate through an examination of Bible passages that Satan's sole power is through temptation, and he has no power to possess a human body.

First, the Creator is God—period. The Bible, and specifically Genesis, are clear about who created the universe. Only God has power over nature. There are very limited occurrences in the Bible, anywhere, of even an angel of God having any power over nature.

Only the prophets (such as Moses) and the disciples, who were given the power to do good works directly from God, Jesus Christ, and the Holy Spirit, were permitted to perform miracles, and all for good. For example, Moses delivered water from the rock at Horeb in Exodus 17, and there are many examples of the disciples performing miracles. In addition, in Genesis 19, when a crowd of people in Sodom wanted to assault the two angels who had visited Lot, the angels "struck the men who were at the door of the house, young and old, with blindness so that they could not find the door" (v. 11). However, aside from clearly God-given powers, no one has power over Creation, with the exception of Satan's ability to influence Job, as described in chapter 8, and his power over the serpent which tempted Eve in Genesis 3.

Satan is described to have at one point been some type of angel equivalent, as described in Revelation 12:7–9:

> Then war broke out in heaven. Michael and his angels fought against the dragon, and the dragon and his angels fought back. But he was not strong enough, and they lost their place in heaven. The great dragon was hurled down—that ancient serpent called the devil, or Satan, who leads the whole world astray. He was hurled to the earth, and his angels with him.

In a clear demonstration of Satan's limitations, Satan was defeated by the Archangel Michael because he was less powerful than Michael. Further, in Hebrews 2:5 we are explicitly told that angels have no power over Creation, "It is not to angels that he has subjected the world to come, about which we are speaking." Therefore, Satan, or any angel or other spiritual being, has no power over Creation, or humankind, who was actually given dominion over Creation by God: "'You made them a little lower than the angels; you crowned them with glory and honor and put everything under their feet.' In putting everything under them, God left nothing that is not subject to him. Yet at present we do not see everything subject to them" (vv. 7–8). These statements indicate that angels, in general, do not have power over Creation and have barely more power than humans. In fact, according to 1 Corinthians 6:3, in heaven humankind will have more power than angels, "Do you not know that we will judge angels? How much more the things of this life!" Human possession by demons would not be consistent with the Bible's descriptions of the powers of angels, of which Satan is a type.

Aside from the Bible's clear description of Satan's lack of power over Creation, the Bible is replete with descriptions of how Satan actually *does* work—namely, through temptation, deceit, and trickery. This is laid out clearly at the very beginning of the Bible, in the story of Adam and Eve from Genesis 3. In describing how Eve sinned, it is written, "Now the serpent was more crafty than any of the wild animals the Lord God had made. He said to the woman, 'Did God really say, "You must not eat from any tree in the garden"?'" (v. 1). Satan tricked Eve using empty, false arguments and lies to convince her to eat from the forbidden tree. He tempted Eve by promising false wisdom and pleasure. However, he did not possess Eve. She ate from the tree of her own free will. Similarly, Adam knew that it was wrong to eat from the forbidden tree, but also allowed himself to be tempted by Satan.

In Paul's second letter to the Corinthians, he reinforces these important points about the fall of Adam and Eve, also explaining to the Corinthians to be watchful for Satan. However, he does not describe demon possession, but rather temptation, deceit, and trickery:

> But I am afraid that just as Eve was deceived by the serpent's cunning, your minds may somehow be led astray from your sincere and pure devotion to Christ. For if someone comes to you and preaches a Jesus other than the Jesus we preached, or if you receive a different spirit from the one you received, or a different gospel from the one you accepted, you put up with it easily enough . . . And no wonder, for Satan himself masquerades as an angel of light. It is not surprising, then, if his servants masquerade as servants of righteousness. Their end will be what their actions deserve. (11:3–4, 14–15)

In 1 Chronicles 21, David is described as sinning against God by conducting a census of Israel:

> Satan rose up against Israel and incited David to take a census of Israel. So David said to Joab and the commanders of the troops, "Go and count the Israelites from Beersheba to Dan. Then report back to me so that I may know how many there are." But Joab replied, "May the Lord multiply his troops a hundred times over. My lord the king, are they not all my lord's subjects? Why does my lord want to do this? Why should he bring guilt on Israel?" (vv. 1–3)

In this description, there is no mention that David was demon-possessed. Rather, he was tempted by Satan to sin against God.

The Bible, and in particular the New Testament, goes into even greater detail about Satan and his ways, and in no case is bodily possession mentioned. For example, in 1 Peter 5:8–9, Peter generally instructs believers to be watchful and resist the devil, through faith, "Be alert and of sober mind. Your enemy the devil prowls around like a roaring lion looking for someone to devour. Resist him, standing firm in the faith, because you know that the family of believers throughout the world is undergoing the same kind of sufferings." While one might read this passage and think that it is vague enough to think that Peter could be speaking about demon possession, one need only remember Peter's very real experiences with sin to understand that he was referring to deception and temptation, rather than demon possession. For example, when Jesus was foretelling the crucifixion and resurrection to his disciples, in order to prepare them for very difficult, but also glorious, times, Peter fell victim to the guile of Satan and rebuked Jesus Christ:

> From that time on Jesus began to explain to his disciples that he must go to Jerusalem and suffer many things at the hands of the elders, the chief priests and the teachers of the law, and that he must be killed and on the third day be raised to life. Peter took him aside and began to rebuke him. "Never, Lord!" he said. "This shall never happen to

you!" Jesus turned and said to Peter, "Get behind me, Satan! You are a stumbling block to me; you do not have in mind the concerns of God, but merely human concerns." Then Jesus said to his disciples, "Whoever wants to be my disciple must deny themselves and take up their cross and follow me." (Matt 16:21–24)

Unfortunately for Peter, this was not the last time he would fall victim to Satan and put distance between himself and Jesus Christ due to his moral, but not physical, weakness:

"Simon, Simon, Satan has asked to sift all of you as wheat. But I have prayed for you, Simon, that your faith may not fail. And when you have turned back, strengthen your brothers." But he replied, "Lord, I am ready to go with you to prison and to death." Jesus answered, "I tell you, Peter, before the rooster crows today, you will deny three times that you know me." (Luke 22:31–34)

Of course, just as Jesus predicted, Satan did in fact "sift" Peter like one would sift wheat, and Peter did deny Jesus three times. These terrible events in Peter's life were undoubtedly branded into his memory. However, they also taught him about the workings and power of Satan, and, like any good leader, Peter, in his first epistle, instructed believers therein.

This excerpt from 1 Peter also explains that Satan is determined, and John, in Revelation 20, describes his endurance and breadth of activities: "When the thousand years are over, Satan will be released from his prison and will go out to deceive the nations in the four corners of the earth—Gog and Magog—to gather them for battle. In number they are like the sand on the seashore" (vv. 7–8). Paul further describes how Satan is clever ("in order that Satan might not outwit us. For we are not unaware of his schemes" [2 Cor 2:11]) and preys on people who are disobedient, proud, or generally weak in faith ("in which you used to live when you followed the ways of this world and of the ruler of the kingdom of the air, the spirit who is now at work in those who are disobedient" [Eph 2:2] and "He must not be a recent convert, or he may become conceited and fall under the same judgment as the devil. He must also have a good reputation with outsiders, so that he will not fall into disgrace and into the devil's trap" [1 Tim 3:6–7]).

Of course, the Bible also makes clear how to fight and overcome Satan, temptation, and evil in general. Many of the authors of the New Testament speak directly to this point. And again, rather than refer to Jesus's or any of the apostles' "exorcisms" or any type of physical exorcism, the only exorcisms to which they refer are spiritual in nature and easily winnable, as long as one has faith in Jesus Christ:

> For our struggle is not against flesh and blood, but against the rulers, against the authorities, against the powers of this dark world and against the spiritual forces of evil in the heavenly realms. Therefore put on the full armor of God, so that when the day of evil comes, you may be able to stand your ground, and after you have done everything, to stand. Stand firm then, with the belt of truth buckled around your waist, with the breastplate of righteousness in place. (Eph 6:12–4)

John clarifies these points numerous times by stating that the whole reason Jesus Christ came to Earth was to overcome sin, death, and Satan, and he was, of course successful, "The one who does what is sinful is of the devil, because the devil has been sinning from the beginning. The reason the Son of God appeared was to destroy the devil's work" (1 John 3:8); and "He seized the dragon, that ancient serpent, who is the devil, or Satan, and bound him for a thousand years" (Rev 20:2).

James iterates this point by explaining that humans, because of the crucifixion and resurrection of Jesus Christ, have absolute power over the devil, as long as one truly believes and has faith in Jesus Christ: "Submit yourselves, then, to God. Resist the devil, and he will flee from you" (Jas 4:7).

Jude elaborates on this idea by explaining that people who are not strong enough in faith, or too haughty to understand their own weaknesses, are susceptible to Satan and ultimately destroy themselves:

> In the very same way, on the strength of their dreams these ungodly people pollute their own bodies, reject authority and heap abuse on celestial beings. But even the archangel Michael, when he was disputing with the devil about the body of Moses, did not himself dare to condemn him for slander but said, "The Lord rebuke you!" Yet these people slander whatever they do not understand, and the very things they do understand by instinct—as irrational animals do—will destroy them. (vv. 8–10).

However, none of these passages in any way refers to or suggests a physical possession by any type of demon or spirit. Rather, they all describe temptation, faith, and spiritual strength and weakness.

The story of Judas Iscariot and his betrayal of Jesus Christ provides the clearest and perhaps most striking illustrations of evil, Satan, and deception for all time. This story also provides a fitting conclusion to this chapter in which I provide Biblical evidence that Satan has no power over Creation, but rather works exclusively through temptation.

Judas Iscariot was one of the twelve original disciples. He was also the person who betrayed the Savior of the world to the chief priests for thirty pieces of silver. It goes without saying that Judas Iscariot performed one of the greatest, if not the greatest, act of evil of all time. However, no one believes that Judas Iscariot was demon-possessed, and he was never described as being demon-possessed. This is despite language such as, in Luke 22, "Then Satan entered Judas, called Iscariot, one of the Twelve." Everyone who reads this sentence knows exactly what Luke meant when he stated that "Satan entered Judas" (v. 3). Luke was not describing the demon possession of Judas. Rather, Luke was explaining that Judas fell victim to temptation, sin, and greed.

Judas was clearly a very weak, immoral person, filled with greed, pride, and Satan. Why would the Gospel writers not have indicated that Judas was demon-possessed? How could such a weak person not have been so easily targeted by Satan for possession? The answer is very simple—Satan does not have the power of physical possession. Satan could not possess Judas's body any more than he could possess the man described in chapter 8 about the miracle of the (Gadarene) demoniac or the man described in chapter 9 about the miracle of the "exorcism" at the Synagogue in Capernaum.

There is one final piece of evidence that Satan cannot directly infiltrate or control a person's mind or body. This proof is the story of the annunciation and nativity of Jesus Christ. Told in Luke 1, the story of the annunciation of the birth of Jesus to Saint Mary by the Angel Gabriel sets forth all of Christianity for all time. This event, though preordained and timeless, establishes that humankind is blessed, because for God to choose to manifest as a human (as we were created in his image) is the greatest blessing of all and the greatest affirmation of the sanctity of humankind. Through this act, humans were given the ability to become one with God, a covenant established from the beginning of time and the Creation, carried forward with the Old Testament patriarchs and prophets, and completed on Earth with the annunciation, nativity, crucifixion and resurrection of Jesus Christ. Therefore, humankind is holy and blessed. And, as promised by Jesus Christ (and further discussed in chapter 12), only by our own free will and rejection of Jesus Christ when we die can we put permanent enmity between us and Jesus Christ and absolve ourselves of the blessing of being human and sharing this blessing with Jesus Christ.

As confirmed in John 1, "The true light that gives light to everyone was coming into the world. He was in the world, and though the world was made through him, the world did not recognize him. He came to that which was his own, but his own did not receive him. Yet to all who did receive him, to those who believed in his name, he gave the right to become children of God—children born not of natural descent, nor of human decision or a husband's will, but born of God. The Word became flesh and made his dwelling among us. We have seen his glory, the glory of the one and only Son, who came from the Father, full of grace and truth" (vv. 9–14). The apostle John confirms that we are, as humans, truly the children of God, share a nature with God, and are therefore holy. Only by our own free will, by rejecting Jesus Christ at the time of our physical death, can we permanently lose this privilege and blessing.

If we are truly holy beings, made in the image of God, in whom God and the Holy Spirit dwell, there would be no possibility for Satan to have any direct influence on our body or soul. As described by Paul in 2 Corinthians 6:15–16, "What harmony is there between Christ and Belial? Or what does a believer have in common with an unbeliever? What agreement is there between the temple of God and idols? For we are the temple of the living God." Only we, by our free will, can fall into temptation and reject Jesus Christ at the last day. Only then would we truly be lost to God. Since Jesus Christ has blessed humankind, so much so that we share a nature with God, Satan cannot infiltrate a person's body or directly control their mind.

In summary, the Bible explains that only God has power over Creation and that Satan works only through temptation, or spiritual demon possession, using tools such as lies, deceit, pride, haughtiness, and trickery. Satan is very powerful, and evil is real. All believers should be mindful and watchful for temptation. But Satan cannot infiltrate a person's body or directly control their mind. This is the promise and the message of the Bible, creation, the fall, Job, and the story of the nativity, crucifixion, and resurrection of Jesus Christ.

CHAPTER 12

What Can the End of the World Tell Us About Demon Possession?

———————

While the other chapters in this book discuss the Bible and mental illness in a more tangible, practical way, this chapter will be substantially more philosophical, theological, and metaphysical. I would like to posit that an exegesis about the end of the world can shed light on the invalidity of demon possession in modern times. While this may seem to be less relevant, I think that this discussion can be particularly instructive and reveal further evidence supporting the thesis of this book.

The end of the world, end of days, or rapture depending on the nomenclature used by one's specific religion, is discussed at length in the Synoptic Gospels (Mark 13, Matthew 24–25, and Luke 21), Revelation, and several New Testament epistles.

In the Gospels, the discussion about the end of times came about while Jesus and several of his disciples (in Mark 13 they are identified as Peter, James, John, and Andrew) were on the Mount of Olives. The disciples asked him about the end of the world: "As Jesus was sitting on the Mount of Olives, the disciples came to him privately. 'Tell us,' they said, 'when will this happen, and what will be the sign of your coming and of the end of the age?'" (Matt 24:3). Jesus describes deception ("Jesus answered: "Watch out that no one deceives you. For many will come in my name, claiming, 'I am the Messiah,' and will deceive many" [vv. 4–5]) and many terrible natural phenomena, such as "wars and rumors of wars" (v. 6), "famines and earthquakes" (v. 7), and "increase of wickedness" (v. 12), and, in general, complete tragedy, desolation, and destruction, "great distress, unequaled from the beginning of the world until now—and never to be equaled again" (v. 21).

Jesus then describes what will happen thereafter:

> Immediately after the distress of those days "the sun will be darkened, and the moon will not give its light; the stars will fall from the sky, and the heavenly bodies will be shaken." Then will appear the sign of the Son of Man in heaven. And then all the peoples of the earth will mourn when they see the Son of Man coming on the clouds of heaven, with power and great glory. And he will send his angels with a loud trumpet call, and they will gather his elect from the four winds, from one end of the heavens to the other. (vv. 29–31)

Jesus then gives a timeline of these events, saying:

> Truly I tell you, this generation will certainly not pass away until all these things have happened. Heaven and earth will pass away, but my words will never pass away. "But about that day or hour no one knows, not even the angels in heaven, nor the Son, but only the Father. As it was in the days of Noah, so it will be at the coming of the Son of Man." (vv. 34–37)

Following this, Jesus describes that the people who will become part of the kingdom of heaven will be like the virgins who faithfully and conscientiously took oil with their lamps, rather than the unfaithful and unprepared virgins who did not take oil, or like the industrious servants who were given talents by their master and gained more talents, rather than the lazy servant who gained no more talents. Finally, Jesus clarifies that he is referring to the judgment of humankind:

> When the Son of Man comes in his glory, and all the an-
> gels with him, he will sit on his glorious throne. All the
> nations will be gathered before him, and he will separate
> the people one from another as a shepherd separates the
> sheep from the goats. He will put the sheep on his right
> and the goats on his left. "Then the King will say to those
> on his right, 'Come, you who are blessed by my Father;
> take your inheritance, the kingdom prepared for you
> since the creation of the world.'" (Matt 25:31–34)

Many people take this discussion relatively literally to mean
that Jesus is referring to his return in a physical sense, establish-
ing a kingdom on Earth, in a physically glorious manner with a
darkened sun and moon, falling stars, etc. They believe that the
thousand years referred to in Revelation 20 ("When the thousand
years are over, Satan will be released from his prison and will go
out to deceive the nations in the four corners of the earth—Gog
and Magog—and to gather them for battle. In number they are like
the sand on the seashore" [vv. 7–8]) is a literal thousand years. This
is generally consistent with the "pre-millennial" schools of thought
about the end of days. So-called "post-millenial" and "amillenial"
schools of thought about the end of days suggest several different
ideas including that Jesus is referring to a spiritual kingdom and
phenomena that were established by his crucifixion and resurrection and less about a literal thousand years. The different schools
of thought also offer different interpretations about when the new
age of Christianity has occurred or will occur, and what they will
consist of. This is unfortunately a relatively substantial source of
disagreement between different sects of Christianity. Fortunately,
there are numerous other references in the Bible about the end of
the world that can reconcile these competing theories.

My personal thinking is some combination of these points of
view. Jesus's description of natural disasters is apocalyptic imagery
used to enhance our understanding of the end of days in a spiritual
sense. Similarly and more importantly, in my opinion, references
to time and kingdoms and the second coming are figurative and
refer less to a physical or spiritual event that will impact the whole

world or any group of people, but definitively refer to one's own life, and, more specifically, death.

For example, Jesus states that these events will happen soon, even before the current generation passes. That this will happen soon is repeated numerous times in the New Testament, including by Peter in his first epistle—"The end of all things is near. Therefore be alert and of sober mind so that you may pray" [1 Pet 4:7]—and by John in the last chapter of Revelation—

> Then he told me, "Do not seal up the words of the prophecy of this scroll, because the time is near. Let the one who does wrong continue to do wrong; let the vile person continue to be vile; let the one who does right continue to do right; and let the holy person continue to be holy." "Look, I am coming soon! My reward is with me, and I will give to each person according to what they have done." (Rev 22:10–12)

A physical rapture per se has not yet occurred. Does that mean that Jesus, Peter, and John were wrong in saying that the end of times was near, and would happen before their generation passed? Of course not. They were referring primarily to our *individual and spiritual* salvation. Namely, our own death and resurrection in Jesus Christ, which are guaranteed to happen soon, and cannot be predicted. This is more important than any physical phenomenon. Interestingly, many atheists and others who try to argue against Christianity use this ostensibly apparent discrepancy of millenialism. Their argument, of course, is moot when Jesus's kingdom and second coming are considered to be spiritual in nature, and the end of times is understood primarily as our individual death and spiritual judgment and resurrection in Jesus Christ.

One may put forth what Paul said in the fourth chapter of his first epistle to the Thessalonians as evidence for a discrete time period for the end of days:

> Brothers and sisters, we do not want you to be uninformed about those who sleep in death, so that you do not grieve like the rest of mankind, who have no hope. For we believe that Jesus died and rose again, and so we

believe that God will bring with Jesus those who have fallen asleep in him. According to the Lord's word, we tell you that we who are still alive, who are left until the coming of the Lord, will certainly not precede those who have fallen asleep. For the Lord himself will come down from heaven, with a loud command, with the voice of the archangel and with the trumpet call of God, and the dead in Christ will rise first. After that, we who are still alive and are left will be caught up together with them in the clouds to meet the Lord in the air. And so we will be with the Lord forever. (vv. 13–17)

To understand this passage again requires an understanding of the context of this passage. The Thessalonians were only newly being introduced to Jesus Christ and were unfamiliar both with his timeless nature, as well as with the nature of salvation. In this passage, Paul is explaining these two related points, Jesus's salvation and victory over death, and that salvation is also timeless, extended for all time, including for those who died before the earthly crucifixion and resurrection of Jesus Christ. These two points are necessarily mutually inclusive, and thus Paul addressed them together. One can imagine that the Thessalonians, and many other early Christians, were quite literally trying to understand, and worried about, what would happen to their beloved family members who died before the crucifixion and resurrection of Jesus Christ on Earth.

Further evidence comes from Paul's first epistle to the Corinthians. In chapter 15, Paul explains that while our beginning is a physical beginning, our ending, namely our death, is spiritual in nature:

So it is written: "The first man Adam became a living being"; the last Adam, a life-giving spirit. The spiritual did not come first, but the natural, and after that the spiritual. The first man was of the dust of the earth; the second man is of heaven. As was the earthly man, so are those who are of the earth; and as is the heavenly man, so also are those who are of heaven. And just as we have borne the image of the earthly man, so shall we bear the image of the heavenly man. I declare to you, brothers and

> sisters, that flesh and blood cannot inherit the kingdom of God, nor does the perishable inherit the imperishable. Listen, I tell you a mystery: We will not all sleep, but we will all be changed—in a flash, in the twinkling of an eye, at the last trumpet. For the trumpet will sound, the dead will be raised imperishable, and we will be changed. (vv. 45–52)

The Bible, and especially Jesus's ministry, were not primarily concerned with physical or natural phenomena such as time, cosmology, geology, or meteorology. Jesus did not die on the cross primarily for earthly or natural reasons. Jesus's concern was fully on our spiritual salvation, and our concern must 100 percent be on believing in him, and avoiding temptation, for now and all time. That was the point of the resurrection—to abolish death and all earthly and worldly attributes of this age, and to enter a communion with him. As described in Hebrews 9:

> For Christ did not enter a sanctuary made with human hands that was only a copy of the true one; he entered heaven itself, now to appear for us in God's presence. Nor did he enter heaven to offer himself again and again, the way the high priest enters the Most Holy Place every year with blood that is not his own. Otherwise Christ would have had to suffer many times since the creation of the world. But he has appeared once for all at the culmination of the ages to do away with sin by the sacrifice of himself. Just as people are destined to die once, and after that to face judgment, so Christ was sacrificed once to take away the sins of many; and he will appear a second time, not to bear sin, but to bring salvation to those who are waiting for him. (vv. 24–28)

There is no mention anywhere in the Bible that we will have an easy life, be healthy, avoid natural disasters, or have any luxury if we believe. We are guaranteed only one thing, the greatest thing, and that is salvation and communion with Jesus Christ, for each person individually, as long as we accept him before we die.

In chapter 9 I referred to the miracle of the paralyzed man whose sins Jesus forgave, as described in Mark 2, Luke 5, and

Matthew 9. When Jesus did this, the Pharisees and other teachers began to think very critically of Jesus, upset that he was, in their opinion, blaspheming God by forgiving sins. Jesus sensed their thoughts and asked them whether they thought that it would be easier to forgive someone's sins or cure their paralysis. In order to demonstrate that Jesus has dominion over all things heavenly and earthly, Jesus then healed the paralytic man, to the amazement of everyone in attendance.

Another example is at the resurrection of Lazarus of Bethany described in John 11. Initially, Jesus and his disciples were sent word by Lazarus's sisters Mary and Martha that Lazarus was ill. Jesus waited two days then decided to go to Judea to "awaken" Lazarus. The disciples told Jesus that it would be good for Lazarus to sleep in order to recover from his illness. They also did not want Jesus to go to Judea out of concern for his safety. They very clearly still did not understand who Jesus really is and why he had to go to Judea. Therefore, Jesus said,

> "Our friend Lazarus has fallen asleep; but I am going there to wake him up." His disciples replied, "Lord, if he sleeps, he will get better." Jesus had been speaking of his death, but his disciples thought he meant natural sleep. So then he told them plainly, "Lazarus is dead, and for your sake I am glad I was not there, so that you may believe. But let us go to him." (vv. 11–15)

Jesus knew that he had to raise Lazarus from the dead to enhance the faith of his disciples whom he would soon leave on Earth and depend upon to continue his ministry of humankind.

When Jesus arrived, he saw how sad everyone was, including the townspeople, Martha, and Mary. To Martha he said,

> "Your brother will rise again." Martha answered, "I know he will rise again in the resurrection at the last day." Jesus said to her, "I am the resurrection and the life. The one who believes in me will live, even though they die; and whoever lives by believing in me will never die. Do you believe this?" "Yes, Lord," she replied, "I believe that you

are the Messiah, the Son of God, who is to come into the world." (vv. 23–27)

Shortly thereafter, Mary said to Jesus, "Lord, if you had been here, my brother would not have died" (v. 32). As the disciples still did not understand who Jesus is, Martha and Mary did not understand the power of Jesus Christ. After being asked to see where Lazarus' body had been placed, "Jesus wept" (v. 35).

These two words are some of the most powerful words in the Bible and some of the most meaningful. After seeing Jesus in tears, the people who were present remarked, "See how he loved him!" (v. 36), implying that Jesus was tearful because he was sad that Lazarus had died. However, the real meaning of Jesus's tears is made apparent by the next four verses:

> But some of them said, "Could not he who opened the eyes of the blind man have kept this man from dying?" Jesus, once more deeply moved, came to the tomb. It was a cave with a stone laid across the entrance. "Take away the stone," he said. "But, Lord," said Martha, the sister of the dead man, "by this time there is a bad odor, for he has been there four days." Then Jesus said, "Did I not tell you that if you believe, you will see the glory of God?" (vv. 37–40)

Jesus was not tearful because he missed Lazarus. What these verses clarify is that Jesus was tearful because the disciples, Martha, Mary, and the townspeople, despite all of Jesus's miracles and everything he had done, still had no understanding of who Jesus is. They were focused on a physical understanding of the situation and of Jesus, rather than on a spiritual understanding.

The relevance of this story to the current discussion is that many times we, believers, fall victim to believing physical phenomena more than the true, supernatural teachings and attributes of Jesus and his message. In this story, Jesus is clearly trying to teach everyone present and who reads the story for all time that healing a paralytic person, or any other physical miracle, is not in and of itself the message of Jesus Christ but meant to enhance the true message, miracle, and story of Jesus Christ—namely, that

Jesus Christ was crucified and rose from the dead on the third day to abolish our sins, thereby giving eternal life to all who believe in him. Of course, Jesus Christ exorcised demons and Satan in the greatest way possible. He allowed himself to be crucified and then resurrected. All other miracles, phenomena, and stories are meant to confirm and lead us to this revelation. The true miracle, or "exorcism" if you will, performed by Jesus is his resurrection and subsequent victory over death, not his casting out of spirits or healing people who are blind or have other physical or mental conditions.

This is true regarding the end of times as well. Earthquakes, famines, and earthly kingdoms are not the focus of the Bible. The message of the Bible is about everyone, *individually*, and how we can achieve salvation before it is too late—i.e., before our physical death. It is not primarily about floods, plagues, the Corinthians, the disciples, gentiles, Romans, Thessalonians, the end of times, or any other specific group or event or natural phenomenon. The Bible is about the crucifixion and resurrection of Jesus Christ and its meaning to each and every human being, individually, who can obtain salvation through them. As stated in the last chapter of the Bible, "I am the Alpha and the Omega, the First and the Last, the Beginning and the End" (Rev 22:13). God is timeless and Jesus Christ is timeless. His crucifixion and resurrection were pre-ordained from before the Creation and are timeless and spaceless. The fall of Adam and Eve, the flood, Sodom and Gomorrah, the disobedience, destruction and captivity of Israel, the Pharisees and Sanhedrin, the Romans, Pontius Pilate, the Herods, the people who stoned Stephen, Peter's denial, the arrogance of the apostles, and the nails with which Jesus Christ were nailed are our sins and the crucifixion of Jesus Christ. The delivery of Israel from the Egyptians, Noah's safe passage in the ark, the defeat of Jericho, the victory of David over Goliath, Daniel's deliverance from the den of lions, the journeys of Paul, Jonah's delivery from the large fish, and the second coming of Jesus Christ are our ultimate salvation from death and the resurrection of Jesus Christ. The second coming of Jesus Christ is now and has always been. The Bible is not about groups of historical peoples but every person individually. Jesus Christ's kingdom and ability to grant salvation are timeless and limitless. There is no "future" salvation for the world in physical terms because God and Jesus Christ's salvation are timeless and always have been. The future is now and about you, me, and every other individual who ever was, is, or will be. This is a requirement of salvation through Jesus Christ. We have been granted the ability to obtain salvation, through grace, though we must make the choice to accept God's grace because our own time is limited by physical death, introduced by the fall of Adam and Eve, which is the only natural barrier to salvation, and forces the end of the world for us all. Only accepting Jesus Christ as our Savior can save us from the end of the world, which is death, and distance from God. This is what needs to be understood about the Bible to fully grasp its meaning. This was summarized in six verses in the Gospel of John:

> For God so loved the world that he gave his one and only Son, that whoever believes in him shall not perish but have eternal life. For God did not send his Son into the world to condemn the world, but to save the world through him. Whoever believes in him is not condemned, but whoever does not believe stands condemned already because they have not believed in the name of God's one and only Son. This is the verdict: Light has come into the world, but people loved darkness instead of light because their deeds were evil. Everyone who does evil hates the light, and will not come into the light for fear that their deeds will be exposed. But whoever lives by the truth comes into the light, so that it may be seen plainly that what they have done has been done in the sight of God. (John 3:16–21)

So how is all of this relevant to the thesis of this book? The physical possession of a human by a demon (or Satan, who, by definition, is the source of all demons) implies not only that Satan has power over Creation, but also that there are limits to our ability as individuals—our free will—to achieve salvation. Demon-possession strips us of our free will and ability to choose to accept

God's grace and forces us to choose evil. It suggests that a physical possession can preclude salvation, or a sort-of "end of the world" that is not our death but some other natural phenomenon over which we have no control. It puts time and space limits on salvation besides our physical death. More substantially, this would imply that there are limits to God's ability to grant salvation. Further, the requirement for exorcisms suggests that our free will, the Holy Spirit within us, and the general revelation of Jesus Christ, may not be adequate to achieve salvation—that there is a point of "no-return" besides our death that cannot be overcome by accepting Jesus Christ, but by practitioners of spiritual healing who, for unclear reasons, are endowed with supernatural powers.

This is not consistent with Christianity. Even the most depraved, evil people on earth, who are not demon-possessed, can very easily be saved in an instant, all by themselves, by truly accepting Jesus Christ before they die. For example, consider the thief on the right of Jesus who was crucified along with Jesus Christ. After the other thief insulted Jesus, the thief on Jesus' right "stole" salvation, as described in Luke 23:

> One of the criminals who hung there hurled insults at him: "Aren't you the Messiah? Save yourself and us!" But the other criminal rebuked him. "Don't you fear God," he said, "since you are under the same sentence? We are punished justly, for we are getting what our deeds deserve. But this man has done nothing wrong." Then he said, "Jesus, remember me when you come into your kingdom." Jesus answered him, "Truly I tell you, today you will be with me in paradise." (vv. 39–43)

No one is beyond redemption. He loves every human being equally. We are all depraved, sinful people. God has never and will never allow Satan to have dominion over our minds or free will. Only we can prevent our own salvation by not accepting Jesus Christ before we die—our individual rapture, end of times, or end of the world. This is the promise and the message of the Bible, Creation, and the crucifixion and resurrection of Jesus Christ.

CHAPTER 13

Conclusion and a Message of Hope

The goal of this book is to help change misconceptions about serious mental illness that have historically pervaded Christianity. In particular, I sought to provide evidence for the following two-part thesis: 1) serious mental illness was present and relatively common in Biblical times, and similar in phenomenology to how it manifests today, and 2) some instances of demon possession and exorcisms as described in the Bible could be better explained by occurring in the context of untreated mental illness using a post-Enlightenment rationale, and that this could reveal a great deal of information about the Biblical view of mental illness.

In the first two chapters, I introduced the concept of serious mental illness, as well as the reasons for why it is so important to make sure that Christian believers understand it. Many people falsely believe that serious mental illness is solely a result of drug use or bad parenting and is exclusive to modern times. Many others, especially religious individuals, believe that serious mental illness is related to demon possession and immorality. Many people simply equate any bad, undesirable, or evil behavior with mental illness. Serious mental illness, though relatively common, is much less common than other forms of mental illness such as anxiety and depression. Individuals with serious mental illness are too often homeless or incarcerated, isolated from society. Those who live on the margins of society and have untreated serious mental illness may be so bizarre as to seem inhuman. It would be hard for most people to identify or empathize with such individuals. Regardless of the etiology, the lack of understanding of serious mental illness contributes to the stigma of serious mental illness and ultimately prevents individuals with serious mental illness from receiving sorely needed professional help.

In chapter 3 I presented how Moses described to Israel serious mental illness, along with physical illness, as a consequence of disobedience to God. For Moses to describe serious mental illness as a consequence of disobedience to God suggests that it must have been so prevalent, devastating, and common that it would have been understood by the common Israelite. Similarly, in chapter 5 I presented how King David feigned psychosis in such a way that was convincing and very recognizable to King Achish and his group, suggesting the relative commonality of this behavior and a general understanding of the presence of psychosis, even if such individuals were perceived as a bother and little could be done.

Chapters 4, 6, and 7 dealt with the symptoms of serious mental illness experienced by King Saul, Jonah, and Nebuchadnezzar, three of the most well-known, important characters in the Bible and people in the history of civilization. These three individuals were also very different. King Saul was God's chosen leader of Israel. Jonah was a great prophet. Nebuchadnezzar was a Babylonian monarch who destroyed Jerusalem. These descriptions were enhanced by discussions of the severe depression, and at times suicidality, experienced by Moses, Naomi, Jeremiah, Job, and Elijah. In addition to illustrating the timelessness of serious mental illness, these stories demonstrate that symptoms of serious mental illness do not discriminate between people based on their race, wealth, profession, social status, or belief in God. Everyone is susceptible to mental illness.

In chapters 8 and 9 I presented two of the miracles of Jesus Christ that are widely described as exorcisms. In both cases I described in detail how considering the behavior of the afflicted individuals in the context of untreated serious mental illness can enhance our understanding of these stories. I described how serious mental illness during the time of Jesus Christ was not understood and indeed still considered to be caused by evil spirits, and that Jesus used era-appropriate, pre-Enlightenment language for these miracles. I used additional examples of how even very clear physical conditions were described using the same language. I reviewed the clear distinction between how potential medical and psychiatric conditions are discussed in the Bible compared to how evil works, Satan, magic, sin, or the devil are discussed. Chapter 8 includes a commentary on the stories of Adam and Eve and Job and how their stories make clear the limited extent to which God allows Satan, the source of all demons and spirits, to affect humankind. Namely, that God has never and will never allow Satan to have dominion over our minds or free will. In other words, Satan, who is the source of all demons and evil spirits, cannot infiltrate a person's mind. This is the promise of the Bible, Creation, the fall, Job, and Jesus Christ.

Chapter 9 includes a direct examination of exorcisms, both in Biblical and modern times. While understanding the story of the miracle of the "exorcism" at the Synagogue in Capernaum in Chapter 9 reveals a great deal about the Biblical understanding of serious mental illness, other phenomena predominate today and lie on a spectrum from pure deceit, malingering, and fakery on one end to other types of conditions that are classified as psychiatric disorders but are quite distinct from serious mental illness, such as factitious and somatic symptom disorders. Chapter 9 ends with a reminder that whether the miracles described in chapters 8 and 9 were exorcisms or miraculous healings of mental illness is relatively unimportant as all miracles are meant to lead us to and enhance our understanding of the true message, miracle, and story of Jesus Christ—namely, that Jesus Christ was crucified and rose from the dead on the third day to abolish our sins, thereby giving eternal life to all who believe in him. I reinforced that of course Jesus Christ exorcised demons and Satan, in the greatest way possible. He allowed himself to be crucified and then resurrected. All other miracles, phenomena, and stories are meant to confirm and lead us to this revelation. The true miracle, or "exorcism" if you will, performed by Jesus is his resurrection and subsequent victory over death, not his casting out of spirits or healing people who are blind or have other physical or mental conditions.

Using examples from both the Old and New Testament, chapter 10 describes how the Bible, in no uncertain way, repeatedly condemns any sort of witchcraft, magic, or related spiritual behavior. The exorcising of demons and anything related to supernatural phenomena are antithetical to what is taught in the Bible, are against God, and are listed among the worst sins, such as murder and idolatry.

In chapter 11, I reviewed how the Bible explains that only God has power over Creation, and that Satan works through temptation, or spiritual demon possession, using tools such as lies, deceit, pride, haughtiness, and trickery. The Bible is clear that Satan is very powerful, and that evil exists. All believers should be mindful and watchful for temptation. However, the Bible is also clear that, since Jesus Christ has blessed humankind, so much so that we share a nature with God, Satan cannot infiltrate a person's body or directly control their mind.

In a substantially more philosophical, theological, and metaphysical chapter than any of the others chapters in this book, chapter 12 presented an exegesis about the end of the world, both metaphorically and literally, and a discussion about how what the Bible says about the end of the world can shed light on the invalidity of demon possession. Chapter 12's conclusion was that demon possession is not consistent with Christianity and actually suggests limitations to our free will and the power and grace of Jesus Christ.

In summary, I have presented evidence from both the Old and New Testaments that, from a post-Enlightenment perspective, clearly indicates that: 1) symptoms of serious mental illness were common and identifiable even by lay people in Biblical times; 2) many people from all walks of life in Biblical times were afflicted with serious mental illness; 3) untreated serious mental illness in Biblical times manifested very similarly to how it manifests today; 4) many examples of demon possession in the Bible can be better explained in the context of serious mental illness, which enhances the messages of these stories; 5) Jesus Christ clearly distinguished between mental illness and actual spirits/demons; 6) Satan and his spirits have no ability to infiltrate or control a person in a direct manner; 7) both physical and mental illness were described in spiritual terms in Biblical times; 8) whether the miracles described in chapters 8 and 9 were exorcisms or miraculous healing of mental illness is relatively unimportant as all miracles are meant to lead us to and enhance our understanding of the true message of Jesus Christ; 9) while many Christian believers also believe in a false equivalence between moral weakness/sin and mental illness, there are no descriptions of a sinful act committed by the people described in the stories of the miracle of the "exorcism" at the Synagogue in Capernaum and the miracle of the (Gadarene) demoniac; 10) witchcraft, magic, the exorcising of demons and anything related to supernatural phenomena are antithetical to what is taught in the Bible; 11) Satan works by temptation; 12) demon possession actually suggests limitations to our free will and the power and grace of Jesus Christ; 13) since Jesus Christ has blessed humankind, so much so that we share a holy nature with God and have the Holy Spirit within us, Satan could never infiltrate a person's body or directly control their mind.

Based on these premises, I submit that my theses that 1) serious mental illness was present and relatively common in Biblical times, and similar in phenomenology to how it manifests today, and that 2) some instances of demon possession and exorcisms as described in the Bible could be better explained by occurring in the context of mental illness, and that this could reveal a great deal of information about the Biblical view of mental illness, follow. However, my goal in this book is not to change the readers' views of the Bible stories presented herein, but rather to use the Bible to enhance what we understand about serious mental illness.

Therefore, the last remaining question is, how much does this really matter? If whether the miracles described in chapters 8 and 9 were exorcisms or miraculous healings of mental illness is relatively unimportant, as all miracles are meant to lead us to and enhance our understanding of the true message of Jesus Christ, why then does it matter whether people still believe in exorcisms or believe that mental illness is caused by evil spirits.

It makes all of the difference. Before the 1950s, the advent of psychopharmacology,[1] and the development of the first psychiatric medications, treatment for severe psychiatric disorders was limited and sometimes barbaric. Insulin-induced seizures, injections of castor oil, and shocking patients' bodies by alternatively submerging them in freezing cold followed by scalding hot water were commonplace. Many of these patients were locked up in insane asylums. Few of these individuals were able to lead any sort of approximation of a normal life.

Psychiatric medications were initially discovered serendipitously, and they had a major impact. Within years and decades after the initial discovery of antipsychotic medications in the mid-twentieth century, many more medications were developed. Thousands of previously chronically institutionalized patients were able to leave the state hospitals and receive treatment as outpatients. Many were able to develop relationships and hold jobs. Regular use of clozapine in America in the late twentieth century further contributed to this revolution in the treatment of psychiatric patients.

Then finally, shortly after the introduction of clozapine, the field learned that the earlier a medication is started for someone with schizophrenia, the better their long-term outcomes.[2] This further revolutionized the treatment of schizophrenia and led to the opening of first-episode and prodromal clinics and research

1. Lehmann and Ban, "History of the Psychopharmacology of Schizophrenia," 152–62.

2. Perkins et al. "Relationship between Duration of Untreated Psychosis and Outcome," 1785–804; Wyatt, "Neuroleptics and the Natural Course of Schizophrenia," 325–51.

programs all across the world. The field has not looked back and is united in its efforts to identify and treat individuals with serious mental illness as early in their illness as possible.

However, the most important factors in the care of any psychiatric patient remain, in the opinion of this author and psychiatrist, the patient and their family. All of the efforts by the psychiatric community and scientific advances are moot if patients and their families do not appreciate the non-morality- and non-spirituality-based biological nature and timelessness of serious mental illness, as well as the necessity and therapeutic potential of currently available treatments. While a very unfortunate minority of patients who receive medications for schizophrenia remain severely disabled, the vast majority substantially improve on medications. However, without medications, many would remain severely disabled. The difference between patients with serious mental illness on versus off of medications is profound and obvious. Medications make all of the difference, and in my experience, the single greatest factor that determines the willingness of a patient to take medications, and therefore their prognosis, is the support of their family. Almost by definition, serious mental illness takes away a patient's insight. Patients with serious mental illness often do not think they are ill. Therefore, family members play a huge role in helping patients with serious mental illness accept treatment. Neither the patients nor their families need to understand the illness except to know that the patient has one and needs medication.

Thinking that one has an illness caused by an evil spirit, or shunning traditional medicine for religious or spiritual healing, would severely jeopardize a patient's chances of recovery. Great strides have been made in the treatment of serious mental illness. The vast majority of people with serious mental illness can lead normal or near normal lives. There is hope and good news for those with serious mental illness and for those with family members with mental illness. Although people in Biblical times did not understand mental illness or have the ability to treat it, post-Enlightenment rationality, scientific advances, and theology have given us the information and evidence we need to understand that serious mental illness is consistent with a Christian worldview and is as old as humankind. And now we can treat mental illness. Therefore, it is up to each of us, as individuals, to take these lessons from the Bible and apply them to our lives.

Mr. S, from chapter 1, eventually matriculated at college in a different state than where his parents live. Since he was alone and away from his parents, he no longer had their support and reminders about taking his medications, and so he stopped them. Within three months, he was taken to an emergency department by police after he was found in the subway station yelling about the imminent judgment of mankind and after having assaulted a bystander whom he thought was Satan. Mr. S had developed schizophrenia.

Mr. S was eventually admitted to a psychiatric hospital and restarted on medications. He made a quick recovery and went back to live with his parents. He reentered college the following year and recently graduated. He also eventually married and has two children. By all accounts, he is living a happy, normal life. He is still taking his medication and sees his psychiatrist every three months. He eventually developed an understanding that his symptoms, including thinking that he receiving messages from angels and that Satan had possessed his cat, had nothing to do with God or Satan, but were symptoms of schizophrenia.

While Mr. S's ultimate outcome was a good one, there are many more patients who do not have the support of their family or do not develop the insight displayed by Mr. S. In addition, Mr. S's hospitalization and act of violence could have potentially been avoided. It is for these reasons why I have written this book, and I am hopeful that I will have made a difference in even one person's life.

Epilogue

There are two final points about serious mental illness and Christianity that are not directly related to the thesis of this book, but are peripherally related and important, and so I would like to address them herein. The first is the phenomenon of "voices," "conversations," and other experiences that Christian believers describe as having with God. Everyone's relationship with God is unique, deep, and spiritual. Many people, when engaged in deep prayer, meditation, or worship, have strong emotional experiences that are spiritually-based and greatly enhance one's faith. People who experience these phenomena may describe them in terms of "hearing God" speaking with them or "having a conversation with God." However, these are very distinct from true psychotic experiences, in six ways: 1) these spiritual experiences are limited to times of worship, prayer, and meditation, whereas true psychotic experiences would generally not be limited to these scenarios; 2) true psychotic experiences are true perceptual, and not just emotional, experiences; that is, a person with psychosis who hears a voice or tastes something that is not real (i.e., a hallucination) is actually hearing something or tasting something that is registering in the relevant areas of their brain, whereas the spiritual experiences of believers are not related to the five senses but are metaphysical and emotional in nature; 3) the symptoms of a psychotic person will generally be associated with severe functional impairment, whereas the spiritual experiences of believers would not be; 4) the symptoms of a psychotic person would often be associated with other psychotic symptoms (e.g., other hallucinations, delusions, or negative symptoms), whereas the spiritual experiences of believers would not be associated with other psychotic experiences; 5) the symptoms of a psychotic person generally begin in the late teens and early twenties, whereas the spiritual experiences of believers could begin at any time; 6) the symptoms of a psychotic person would respond to treatment, whereas the spiritual experiences of believers would not respond to treatment. Therefore, these personal emotional experiences do not indicate mental illness and can be very normal experiences that can enhance one's relationship with God.

Importantly, these sorts of experiences must also be clearly distinguished from people who supposedly receive divine instructions to murder, kill, or otherwise harm people. In very rare instances, these people may have bona fide psychiatric illness, in which case they would need institutionalization and intense psychiatrist treatment. In many cases, these individuals are not telling the truth about their experiences.

The second point, about which I am very frequently asked by my patients, is whether people with serious mental illness, such as psychotic disorders, or other disorders that ravage a person's mind, such as Alzheimer's disease, and can make a person act in a very sinful way or just ignore Jesus Christ, can be saved. The answer is, in my opinion, an unambiguous yes.

Serious mental illness, such as schizophrenia, can so overwhelm a person that they are fully engaged in their psychotic experiences, essentially ignoring or forgetting Jesus Christ. In other situations, psychotic individuals may feel that Jesus Christ, God, or the church is an enemy or alien invader. Others may believe they are Satan. And yet others, though extremely rare, may receive command auditory hallucinations, often believing them to be from God, to kill people, and act on them. Similarly, individuals with dementing illnesses, such as Alzheimer's disease, often undergo complete personality changes. Sometimes men or women who have been married for many decades develop Alzheimer's disease, begin living in nursing homes, forget their spouses, and develop relationships with people in the nursing homes. Besides being extremely distressing to family members, people are often concerned that this sort of sinful behavior will lead to their condemnation and prevent their salvation.

This is not true, for two reasons. Most importantly, salvation comes from grace. All humankind is sinful and flawed, and there is no act or amount of acts that can earn salvation. Salvation comes from Jesus Christ and the cross alone.

The second reason does get to the crux of this book. As described above, mental illness is non-spirituality and non-morality-based, and biological in nature. No one has control over such conditions. God obviously understands this and would naturally understand that sinful behaviors that are the result of mental illness are not actually the result of evil or sin, but the result of an illness, not temptation and certainly not "demon possession." While we can only see what is on the outside of people, God can see what is on the inside. He could see what was on the inside of King Saul, Nebuchadnezzar, Jonah, the (Gadarene) demoniac, and the man who was "exorcised" at the Synagogue in Capernaum. And as was demonstrated by these stories, God loves everyone and gives everyone a chance at salvation, including those afflicted with serious mental illness who are otherwise too impaired to understand things the way that individuals without such severe conditions would.

These points are further illustrated by similar questions people have about other extraordinary circumstances, such as what happens to babies who die shortly after childbirth, or to people who live on remote islands and have never heard of Jesus Christ. As Christians, we believe that God's revelation is universal. In the case of young babies who die shortly after childbirth, we as Christians believe that they could be saved by grace, because of their extremely limited knowledge of right and wrong and inability for agency or responsibility both in terms of accepting Jesus Christ, but also in terms of acting against Jesus Christ.

In the case of people who live on remote islands and have never heard of Jesus Christ, they also have the opportunity to be saved. They too are saved by grace and the general revelation of Jesus Christ—namely, his revelation in nature, conscience, and providence. As described in Romans 1:18–20:

> The wrath of God is being revealed from heaven against all the godlessness and wickedness of people, who suppress the truth by their wickedness, since what may be known about God is plain to them, because God has made it plain to them. For since the creation of the world God's invisible qualities—his eternal power and divine nature—have been clearly seen, being understood from what has been made, so that people are without excuse.

The general revelation is also revealed in Psalm 19:1–6—

> The heavens declare the glory of God; the skies proclaim the work of his hands. Day after day they pour forth speech; night after night they reveal knowledge. They have no speech, they use no words; no sound is heard from them. Yet their voice goes out into all the earth, their words to the ends of the world. In the heavens God has pitched a tent for the sun. It is like a bridegroom coming out of his chamber, like a champion rejoicing to run his course. It rises at one end of the heavens and makes its circuit to the other; nothing is deprived of its warmth.

—and Matthew 5:45—

> that you may be children of your Father in heaven. He causes his sun to rise on the evil and the good, and sends rain on the righteous and the unrighteous.

Further, God judges people differently, based on their faculties and general understanding of, and exposure to, Jesus Christ, as described in Luke 12:47–48:

> The servant who knows the master's will and does not get ready or does not do what the master wants will be beaten with many blows. But the one who does not know

and does things deserving punishment will be beaten with few blows. From everyone who has been given much, much will be demanded; and from the one who has been entrusted with much, much more will be asked.

A baby and a person on a remote island would all classify as "one who does not know" based on their abilities or experiences to "know," and would be judged accordingly.

Therefore, people with serious mental illness, such as psychotic disorders, or other disorders that ravage a person's mind, such as Alzheimer's disease, and could potentially make a person act in a very sinful way or just ignore Jesus Christ, have equal chance of being saved as anyone else. God does not have favorites, is all-knowing, and loves every human being equally. His grace has no boundaries, and he understands the impact of serious mental illness.

Bibliography

American Psychiatric Association. *Diagnostic and Statistical Manual of Mental Disorders*. 5th ed. Washington, DC: American Psychiatric Association, 2013.

Fusar-Poli, Paolo, et al. "The Psychosis High-risk State: A Comprehensive State-of-the-art Review." *JAMA Psychiatry* 70.1 (2013) 107–20.

Heckers, S. "Bleuler and the Neurobiology of Schizophrenia." *Schizophrenia Bulletin* 37.6 (2011) 1131–5.

Hjorthoj, Carsten, et al. "Years of Potential Life Lost and Life Expectancy in Schizophrenia: a Systematic Review and Meta-analysis." *The Lancet Psychiatry* 4.4 (2017) 295–301.

Kane, John, et al. "Clozapine for the Treatment-resistant Schizophrenic: A Double-blind Comparison with Chlorpromazine." *Arch Gen Psychiatry* 45.9 (1988) 789–96.

Keller, Jennifer, et al. "Current Issues in the Classification of Psychotic Major Depression." *Schizophr Bull.* 33.4 (2007) 877–85.

Lehmann, H. E., and T. A. Ban. "The History of the Psychopharmacology of Schizophrenia." *Can J Psychiatry* 42.2 (1997) 152–62.

Lieberman, J. A. First MB. "Psychotic Disorders." *N Engl J Med.* 379.3 (2018) 270–80.

Mann, J. John "The Medical Management of Depression." *N Engl J Med.* 353.17 (2005) 1819–34.

Perkins, D. O., et al. "Relationship between Duration of Untreated Psychosis and Outcome in First-episode Schizophrenia: A Critical Review and Meta-analysis." *Am J Psychiatry* 162.10 (2005) 1785–804.

Substance Abuse and Mental Health Services Administration. "Key Substance Use and Mental Health Indicators in the United States: Results from the 2018 National Survey on Drug Use and Health." https://store.samhsa.gov/system/files/pep19-5068.pdf.

Bibliography

Wyatt, R. J. "Neuroleptics and the Natural Course of Schizophrenia." *Schizophr Bull.* 17.2 (1991) 325–51.